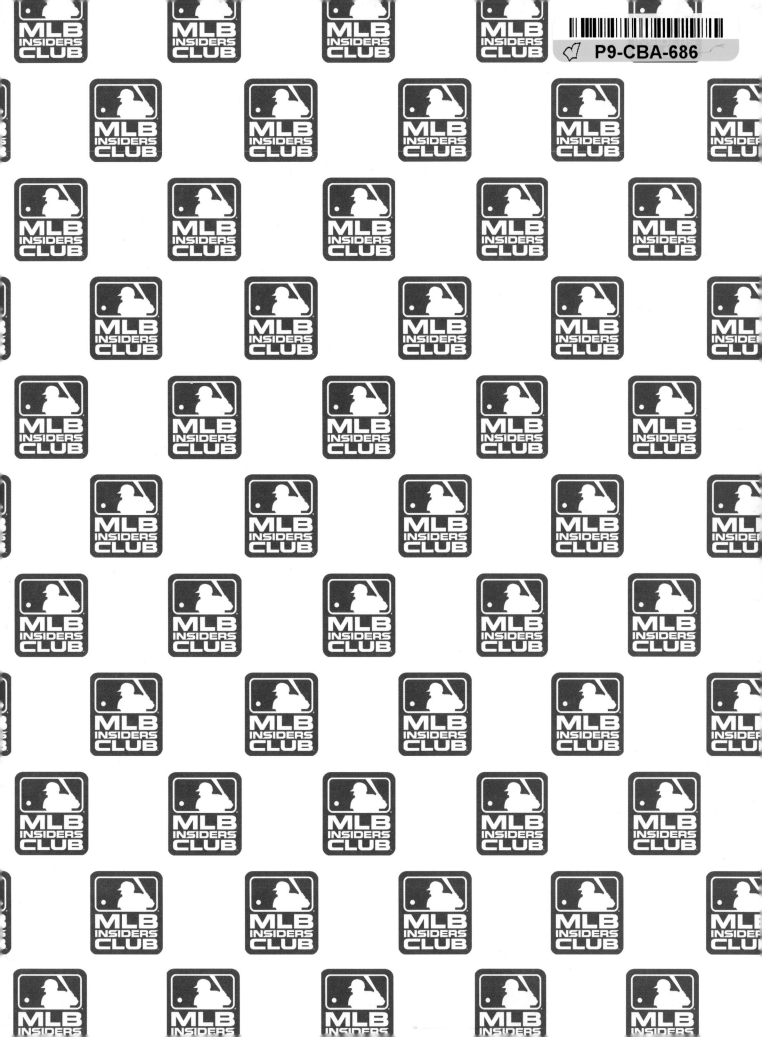

BASEBALL'S
GREATEST
GAMES

The most suspenseful, exciting and unforgettable contests in Major League Baseball history.

Baseball Insiders Library™

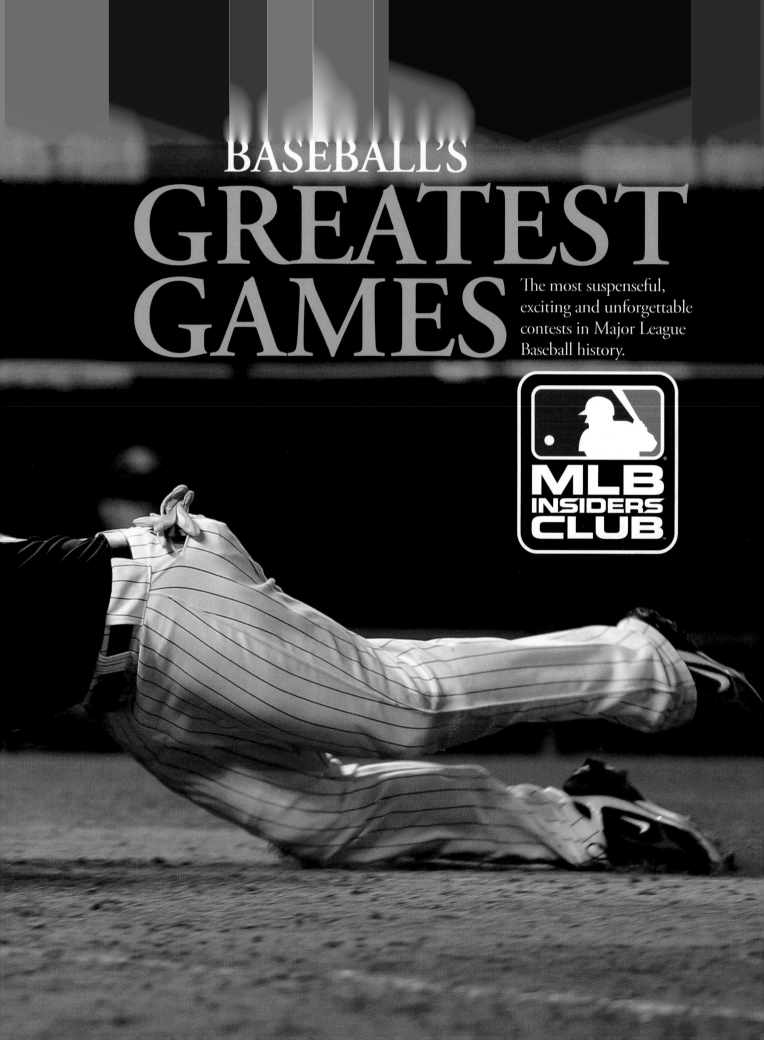

BASEBALL'S
GREATEST
GAMES

The most suspenseful, exciting and unforgettable contests in Major League Baseball history.

MLB INSIDERS CLUB

BASEBALL'S GREATEST GAMES by Eric Enders

The most suspenseful, exciting and unforgettable contests in Major League Baseball history.

Printed in 2009

About the Author

Eric Enders is a freelance writer whose work has appeared in The New York Times *and many other publications. A former historian at the Baseball Hall of Fame in Cooperstown, he is the author of* Ballparks Then and Now *and* The Fall Classic: The Definitive History of the World Series. *He lives in El Paso, Texas, where he operates Triple E Productions, a baseball research service.*

Major League Baseball Properties

Vice President, Publishing
Donald S. Hintze

Editorial Director
Mike McCormick

Publications Art Director
Faith M. Rittenberg

Senior Production Manager
Claire Walsh

Associate Editor
Jon Schwartz

Associate Art Director
Melanie Posner

Senior Publishing Coordinator
Anamika Chakrabarty

Project Assistant Editors
Chris Greenberg, Jodie Jordan

Editorial Intern
Karl de Vries

Major League Baseball Photos

Director
Rich Pilling

Photo Editor
Paul Cunningham

MLB Insiders Club

Creative Director
Tom Carpenter

Managing Editor
Jen Weaverling

Prepress
Wendy Holdman
Gina Germ

MLB Insiders Club
12301 Whitewater Drive
Minnetonka, MN 55343

TABLE OF CONTENTS

INTRO

DO WALK-OFF HOME RUNS MAKE A BASEBALL GAME great? Or is it memorable performances by the game's stars? Perhaps it's about the circumstances, or the stage of the World Series. It can be a dramatic stolen base or a come-from-behind rally. It can be the beauty of an artful pitching performance or a brutal offensive onslaught. It can be the look of amazement on the faces of players and fans alike after an unbelievable play in the field. It can be a single at-bat in which nothing else matters but the showdown between pitcher and hitter — think Bob Welch against Reggie Jackson. Truth be told, just about any of these things *could* make a game great. Yet there is no recipe for greatness. After all, most games are not great. They may be compelling and exciting, but greatness remains an elusive achievement.

A truly great game, one that will stand the test of time and become a touchstone for generations of ballplayers and fans, never could be reduced to such concrete things. A great game is always more than the sum of its parts. It's about much more than the home run or the stolen base that decided the outcome. It's more than the names of the players involved. And it's even more than the situation, although an October date always helps. With thousands of games played throughout the course of hundreds of seasons, there are hundreds of thousands of games in the baseball canon. Yet only a fraction of those have the right combination of the aforementioned elements and enough ephemeral magic to be considered one of baseball's *greatest* games.

With more than a century in the record books and scrap-books, fans have formed deep emotional attachments to teams and players. Therefore, the definition of a great game can be highly personal. Cubs fans will crow about a game from 1906 and Cardinals fans will holler about the Ozzie Smith homer in 1985. Others may talk about the first Major League game they ever saw or about the first time they watched their favorite player live, in the ballpark. In 2007, *Sports Illustrated* writer Tom Ver-ducci, when asked to pick the greatest game he had ever seen, reeled off memories from Kirk Gibson to Bill Buckner to Joe Carter. But Verducci selected the time he watched his 10-year-old son's youth team come from three runs behind to win a play-off contest. "Because this was my team and my son and these boys were at the sweet spot of childhood — the wonder years, before cynicism grows — it made this the greatest game I ever saw," he wrote.

Although such personal memories are undeniably powerful, there's nothing that can equal the collective moments of joy and heartache shared among a ballpark full of fans. You know a game has entered the realm of the legendary when only a couple of words are needed to describe it: The Fisk Game. The Mazeroski Game. Truly great games become part of baseball's shorthand lan-guage. For an earlier era, The Snodgrass Game and The Merkle Game required no explanation. They will all be retold in these pages, so those who were there can relive the memories, and those who weren't can imagine they had been.

chapter 1

DEBUTS

A player's Major League debut remains etched in his memory for all time, whether it's the ecstatic kind experienced by Mark Kiger or the nightmarish sort suffered by Adam Greenberg. Oakland's Kiger became the first player to make his debut in the postseason when he played in Game 3 of the 2006 ALCS. The Cubs' Greenberg was beaned badly on the first Big League pitch he saw in 2005. Although that was hardly the type of start he could have imagined, Greenberg's name will still be in the record books. Despite the outcome, Big League debuts usually prove to be unforgettable.

ANDRUW JONES OCTOBER 20, 1996

BY 1996, THE ATLANTA BRAVES HAD ESTABLISHED THEMSELVES AS the decade's most consistently excellent franchise, thanks mostly to a star-producing farm system. In the midst of a run that would see them qualify for 14 consecutive postseasons, the Braves had relied on homegrown players like Tom Glavine, Steve Avery, David Justice, Mark Wohlers, Ryan Klesko and Javy Lopez. As the 1996 postseason loomed, Andruw Jones, possibly the most highly touted prospect in the team's history, joined the list. Hailing from the Caribbean island of Curaçao, Jones had been scouted by the Braves at age 15 and signed at 16 for a mere $46,000.

A hero in his home country by the time of his call-up, the prodigy earned a promotion from Triple-A to the Bigs in August, and the Braves immediately inserted him in their hitting-starved lineup. Although the 19-year-old Jones struggled at the plate, he dazzled in the field, and after sitting for the onset of the playoffs, he was back in the lineup for Games 3 and 7 of the NLCS. It was during Game 1 of the World Series against the Yankees, however, that Jones truly announced his arrival. In his Fall Classic debut, the outfielder homered twice (both on 3-2 counts) to lead his team to a 12-1 victory. In the process, he replaced legendary Yankee Mickey Mantle as the youngest player to homer in a World Series. Jones also became the second player to go long in his first two Series at-bats. "It's pretty special for a kid to do what he did," said the Yankees' Darryl Strawberry, once a teenage prodigy himself. "He's a tremendous player," marveled teammate Chipper Jones. "At 19, he looks like he should be here. Even at 16, he looked like he belonged here."

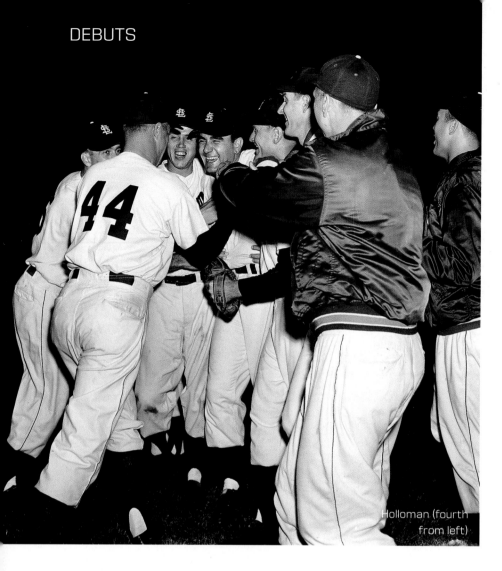

Holloman (fourth from left)

BOBO HOLLOMAN MAY 6, 1953

ON MAY 6, 1953, ALVA "BOBO" HOLLOMAN PROVED THAT ON ANY given night, even the most mediocre pitcher can throw like a Hall of Famer. A 30-year-old career Minor Leaguer in '53, Holloman was a rookie with the St. Louis Browns, who at first had threatened to cut him because he was — as Manager Marty Marion not so gently put it — "too fat." Desperate for arms, however, they opted to keep him on the roster. After Holloman pitched quite poorly in four relief appearances, Marion still decided to give him the start on a wet night when the game against the lowly Philadelphia A's appeared likely to be rained out anyway. As it turned out, the game was played amid a steady downpour with no delays.

Holloman's greatest asset as a pitcher seemed to be his confidence. As Marion put it, "That boy sure believes in himself, and he doesn't mind telling you about it." As Holloman walked to the mound, he followed his usual practice of scratching the initials of his wife and 6-year-old son in the dirt. What he did next, however, was unusual, at least for him. He pitched the game of his life, sinker after sinker finding their way into fielders' gloves. By the time the night was over, he had become the first pitcher since 1892 to throw a no-hitter in his first Big League start. He also drove in three of the Browns' six runs. When the game ended, however, he would turn back into a pumpkin, finishing the season with a 3-7 record and 5.23 ERA, and never pitching in the Major Leagues again.

DETROIT TIGERS
APRIL 25, 1901

BY 1901, THE DETROIT TIGERS were in their eighth season of existence but their first as a Major League club. The city's previous Big League team, the Detroit Wolverines, had folded after the 1888 season. The Tigers debuted in 1894 as a member of the nation's top minor league, the Western League. By 1901 the Western League had renamed itself the American and made a successful bid to gain Major League status by luring many of baseball's elite players away from the National League.

On April 25, 1901, professional baseball returned to Detroit as the Tigers hosted the Milwaukee Brewers. The fans responded very enthusiastically, as the 8,500-capacity Bennett Park was filled to the brim for the opener. The excess fans crammed into standing space behind ropes in the outfield, and play had to be stopped several times as the throng drifted too close to the players.

The home team got off to a horrendous start, committing seven errors (including three by shortstop Kid Elberfeld) and entered the bottom of the ninth inning trailing, 13-4. Many fans gave up on the game and began heading for home on their bicycles or in their buggies. Remarkably, the Tigers exploded for a dramatic finish, scoring 10 runs in the bottom of the ninth inning to win the game. The winning hit was a walk-off double by first baseman Pop Dillon, who was carried off the field by six men, surrounded by the fans who remained.

WILL CLARK APRIL 8, 1986

IN 1985, WILL CLARK, MAYBE THE MOST HERALDED draft pick in Giants history, homered in his very first professional at-bat, on his first swing, with Minor League Fresno. Of course, no one was too surprised. "Will the Thrill" had been crushing the ball since high school in New Orleans. An All-American and a winner of the Golden Spikes Award — given to the collegiate player who shows great ability as well as exceptional sportsmanship — while at Mississippi State, Clark was also a member of the 1984 U.S. Olympic baseball team and batted .429 with three homers and eight RBI during the tournament. He easily won the Giants' first base job in Spring Training before the 1986 season.

On April 8, Clark was penciled into the lineup for his Major League debut against Astros ace Nolan Ryan, the flamethrowing Texan who had struck out more than 200 batters the previous season. "I get up there, and his first pitch is a curveball strike," Clark recalled. The rookie started giggling, amused that the world's fastest pitcher would start him off with a curve. "The next pitch missed, but the next one was a heater, and I zipped it out to center field." Duplicating his Minor League feat, Clark had once again homered on his first career swing. Clark would also homer off of Bob Knepper — also of the Astros — in his debut at Candlestick Park less than a week later. Quickly a fan favorite, sporting his trademark eye black and white-knuckle style of play, Clark's auspicious debuts were only the start of a great career.

DEBUTS

BILL DUGGLEBY APRIL 21, 1898

ON APRIL 21, 1898, PHILLIES HURLER BILL DUGGLEBY made his Major League debut — but it wasn't his pitching that made news. In the second inning, with Philadelphia already trailing, 3-0, Duggleby stepped up to the plate with the bases loaded and became the first player to hit a grand slam in his very first Major League at-bat. He ended up pitching a complete game, holding New York to just one more run in a 13-4 victory. Duggleby would last eight seasons with the Phillies, also pitching a handful of games for the Pirates and Athletics. But as it turned out, he hit like a typical pitcher, turning in a career average of just .165 with six homers. For more than a century, though, he remained the only man to hit a grand slam in his first Big League at-bat. Jeremy Hermida and Kevin Kouzmanoff du-plicated the feat in 2005 and 2006, respectively.

GLOVE WORN
BY DUGGLEBY

PETE GRAY APRIL 17, 1945

AS WORLD WAR II DRAGGED ON, TEAMS LOOKED TO non-traditional sources to replace stars serving overseas. The clubs clamored for players too young or too old to fight, as well as Minor Leaguers, who suddenly found themselves with Big League opportunities. The defending AL champion St. Louis Browns took things a step further when they placed one-armed outfielder Pete Gray on their 1945 Opening Day roster. Gray had had most of his right arm

14

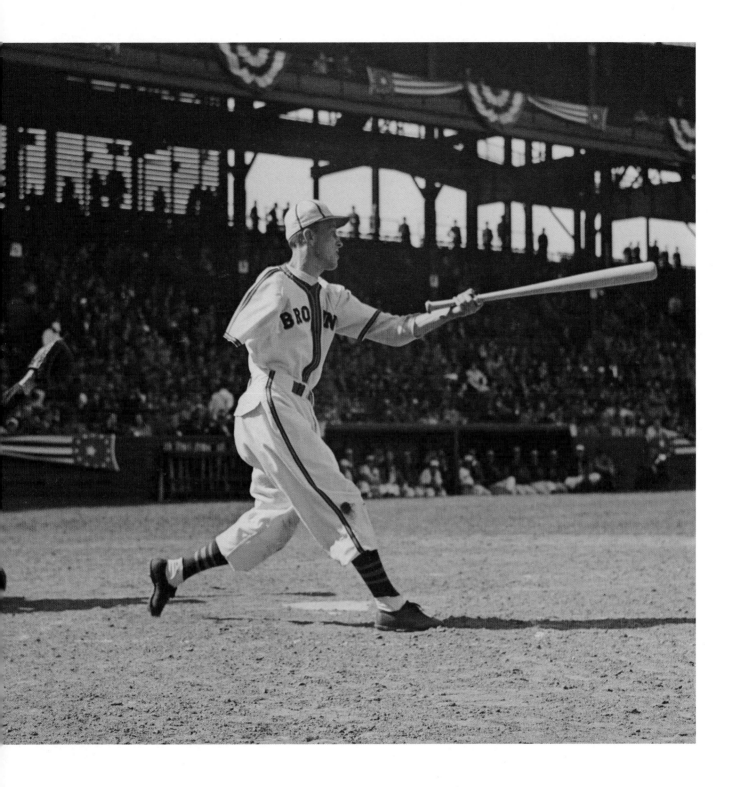

amputated at age 6 after a wagon accident. He still followed his base-ball dream, however, perfecting a one-handed swing (from the left side of the plate) and a fielding maneuver, in which he tucked his glove under the stump of his right arm and pulled the ball out to throw.

Gray had been Most Valuable Player of the Southern League in 1944, batting .333 and tying the league record with 68 sto-len bases. In his Big League debut, he beat out an infield hit

and smacked what seemed to be a sure double until the ball was caught by Tigers center fielder Doc Cramer to the displeasure of the crowd. Soon, however, it became clear that Gray was suscep-tible to the same problem that plagued rookies of all stripes: He couldn't hit the curveball. Gray batted just .218 and never saw action in the Bigs again. Nonetheless, he played well enough to prove that he was no sideshow act.

chapter 2

OPENING DAY

October provides the more memorable thrills, but no day during the baseball season finds fans as unabashedly happy as Opening Day. It's that joyous afternoon when the grass is green, flowers bloom anew, and every team is tied for first. It's that optimistic morning when every manager believes he's headed for the playoffs and every hitter thinks he has a shot at the batting title. And most of all, it's that day when fans, often with a wink and a nod, offer up their most creative excuses to teachers and bosses before heading to the ballpark.

BOB FELLER APRIL 16, 1940

WITH PITCHERS STILL BUILDING UP THEIR WORKLOADS AND getting their bodies and arms into shape, Opening Day is not traditionally known for virtuoso mound performances. But then, Bob Feller was not your average pitcher. Cleveland's ace almost from the moment he stepped on the mound, he proved it with a 5-1 win at age 20 in his first career Opening Day start in 1939. But it was 1940 when he threw the first Opening Day no-hitter.

Frigid temperatures resulted in just 14,000 fans filing into Chicago's Comiskey Park; that included Feller's mother, father and 11-year-old sister, who had traveled from Iowa. "With a raw wind coming in off Lake Michigan," he later told *The New York Times*, "it got colder pretty fast." Feller fanned a relatively modest eight White Sox batters and, true to his wild form, walked five as his team staked him to a 1-0 lead. With two outs in the ninth, it was future Hall of Famer Luke Appling standing between Feller and his no-hit bid. Known for skillfully fouling off tough pitches, Appling wasted four balls before Feller decided "just to get rid of him." The walk Feller issued brought up Taft Wright, who would bat .337 that year. He pulled a hard grounder between first and second, but Indians second baseman Ray Mack managed to keep the ball in the infield, and picked it up in time to retire Wright at first. Through 2008, Feller's no-hitter has remained the only such gem ever thrown on Opening Day.

FELLER'S
NO-HIT BALL

FERNANDO VALENZUELA
APRIL 9, 1981

WHEN JERRY REUSS, THE DODGERS' scheduled starter, pulled a muscle just 48 hours before Opening Day in 1981, the team was left with little choice but to give the emergency start to a 20-year-old rookie, Fernando Valenzuela. Already the youngest player in the Major Leagues, he became the youngest man to get an Opening Day start since Catfish Hunter 15 years earlier. Called up as a reliever the previous September, Valenzuela had an ERA of 0.00 in 17.2 innings — a stretch of debut dominance that would not be echoed until Yankees rookie Joba Chamberlain took the AL by storm in 2007.

Although he had never started a Major League game, Valenzuela had the poise and repertoire of a veteran, baffling the Astros with a mixture of fastballs, sliders and his signature screwball. The rookie tossed a five-hit shutout, striking out Houston's Dave Roberts to end the game. "I knew how much it meant and how much of an honor it was for me," the soft-spoken Valenzuela said through an interpreter. "And it made me nervous for a few minutes. But once I get on the mound, I don't know what the word 'afraid' means." Kept in the rotation for the remainder of the season, Valenzuela became a sensation. He hurled eight straight complete-game victories, including five shutouts. By mid-May he was 8-0 with a 0.50 ERA, and "Fernandomania" was a phenomenon. He ended that season as the only player to win the Cy Young and Rookie of the Year awards in the very same campaign, leading the Dodgers to the world championship to boot.

Cross

PHILLIES VS. BEANEATERS
APRIL 19, 1900

ALTHOUGH 1900 WAS A TIME FOR looking ahead to the 20th century, in baseball it was the last hurrah of an era. In 1901, the American League would rise to Major League status and the National League would institute the foul strike rule, ushering the game into its modern form. The 1900 season was a glorious last gasp for the old style of play.

A game played on April 19, 1900, was the exact opposite of what fans would come to expect in the Deadball Era that was set to begin. The Boston Beaneaters and Philadelphia Phillies combined for 36 runs on 44 hits. The Phillies jumped all over Boston pitcher Vic Willis, a future Hall of Famer, and by the bottom of the seventh they led, 16-4. The onslaught included an unlikely home run by Phils shortstop Monte Cross, whose career slugging percentage of .314 is the 10th-worst of all time.

Boston's Buck Freeman — whose 25 homers the previous year nearly surpassed the single-season record — inexplicably began the game on the bench. But with his team trailing, 17-8, Freeman pinch-hit to lead off the bottom of the ninth and smacked a ball so far over the right-field fence that it reached the other side of a neighboring street. Freeman's homer sparked a nine-run rally that tied the game, 17-17. The Beaneaters' joy was brief, though, as they lost, 19-17, in one of the most thrilling Opening Days ever.

chapter 3
INDIVIDUAL PERFORMANCE: AT THE PLATE

In baseball's early days, home run hitters were often mocked. In 1900, the editors of the Spalding Guide *wrote that an intelligent singles hitter was "worth a dozen of your common class of home-run hitters." But soon Babe Ruth came along and fans flocked to him. Although Babe's power may have changed the game's dimensions, hitting is still a matter of streaks, superstitions and patience. A burst of hot hitting always seems elusive — often disappearing as quickly as it arrived. The Red Sox's George Scott said it best: "When you're hitting the ball, it comes at you looking like a grapefruit. When you're not, it looks like a black-eyed pea."*

section 1: home runs

REGGIE JACKSON OCTOBER 18, 1977

IN THE FRANTIC AND SWELTERING SUMMER OF 1977, the most unforgettable man in New York was still Reggie Jackson. In his first season with the Yankees, Jackson put up MVP-type numbers (32 homers, 110 RBI), and also proved he could do the small things by playing a stellar right field and going 17 for 20 in stolen base attempts. But "The Straw that Stirred the Drink" topped even himself that fall.

With the Yanks leading the Dodgers 3-games-to-2 in the Series, they returned to the Bronx for Game 6. After walking on four pitches his first time up against the Dodgers' Burt Hooton, Jackson came up in the fourth with his team down, 3-2, and the tying run on first. He smacked Hooton's first offering — described by Dodgers Manager Tommy Lasorda as "a fastball with nothin' on it" — into the right-field stands to give the Yanks the lead. Next time up, in the fifth, reliever Elias Sosa threw Jackson a low and outside fastball that he managed to pull over the right-field fence. By the time he got up again in the eighth, the Yanks had a 7-3 lead, and Dodgers knuckleballer Charlie Hough was on the mound. Hough's first knuckler didn't have quite enough dance, and Reggie launched it an estimated 450 feet to center. Three swings, three home runs. Yankee Stadium erupted as Jackson rounded the bases, and the stunned Dodgers players watched with their mouths agape. "I must admit," Steve Garvey said, "when Reggie Jackson hit his third home run and I was sure nobody was listening, I applauded into my glove." Usually brash, Jackson reacted with modesty — despite tying Babe Ruth's record of five homers in a World Series. "Babe Ruth was great," he said. "I'm just lucky."

WILLIE MAYS APRIL 30, 1961

COMING INTO THE FINALE OF A THREE-GAME SERIES against the Braves on April 30, 1961, Willie Mays' confidence was at a low. He was 0 for 7 in the series, including two strikeouts in the first game against Warren Spahn, who threw a no-hitter against Mays' Giants. "When the game started, I didn't feel I would come out of my slump," Mays said of facing Milwaukee's other ace, Lew Burdette. "But on my first time at-bat, I was seeing the ball better." Was he ever. In both the first and third innings, Mays hit long home runs off Burdette, helping the Giants to a 4-3 lead. By the time he came up again in the fifth inning, Burdette had been knocked out and colorful reliever Moe Drabowsky was on the mound. Mays lined out to center, but in the sixth he came up and blasted a monstrous three-run homer off lefty Seth Morehead. Mays' third homer of the day cleared the left-field bleachers and left County Stadium entirely, giving the Giants an 11-3 lead.

He wasn't done though, Mays' fourth homer came off relief ace Don McMahon in the eighth and gave the Giants their final winning margin of 14-4. It looked as if Mays might get a shot at hitting No. 5, but he was stranded on deck in the top of the ninth when Jim Davenport grounded out to end the inning. Still, the four home runs — hit on a sinker and three sliders — were enough for Mays to call it "easily the greatest day I ever had," topping even the day he made his legendary catch in the 1954 World Series. "I don't know what happened to me," he said. "I was just up there swinging."

Lowe (left),
Lou Gehrig

BOBBY LOWE MAY 30, 1894

BOSTON RED SOX FANS WILL ALWAYS REMEMBER DEREK LOWE'S postseason pitching in '04, but they may be surprised to learn he was not Boston's first baseball hero with that surname. That honor belongs to Bobby Lowe of the Boston Beaneaters (now the Atlanta Braves), the most unlikely man to hit four homers in one game. The second baseman and leadoff batter was a mediocre hitter for most of his career. But in 1894, he put up career highs in batting average (.346), hits (212), runs (158), RBI (115) and slugging percentage (.520). Despite those gaudy season totals, it was a single performance in May for which he would be remembered.

After going 0 for 6 in the first game of a Decoration Day (now Memorial Day) doubleheader, Lowe caught fire in the second game against the Reds' Icebox Chamberlain. With its home field under repair, Boston had temporarily moved to the Congress Street Grounds, where the left-field fence stood at just 250 feet. Lowe hit four balls over the fence — including two in one inning — to become the first major leaguer to homer four times in a game. He also added a single for good measure. Chamberlain pitched a complete game despite allowing 19 hits and 18 earned runs, and Boston eventually won, 20-11. Afterward, Beaneater fans showered the field with about $160 in honor of Lowe's game.

MIKE SCHMIDT
APRIL 17, 1976

YOU DON'T NEED TO BE EARL Weaver to figure out that if a player hits four homers in a game, his team usually wins. But as the Phils' Mike Schmidt proved in '76, sometimes each one matters. Schmidt started the year cold, going 3 for 18 and swinging so feebly that Manager Danny Ozark bumped him from third to sixth in the lineup for the first game of a series at Wrigley Field. "Mike, you've got to relax," teammate Dick Allen told the pressing Schmidt. "Baseball ought to be fun. Enjoy it. Be a kid again."

The Friendly Confines featured perfect hitting weather on April 17 — sunny with the wind blowing out — but it seemed to help only the Cubs, who led, 13-2, in the fifth. Schmidt, who flied out and singled in his first two at-bats, hit a two-run shot off Rick Reuschel his next time up, making it 13-4. Two innings later he homered off Reuschel again, with the bases empty. By the time Schmidt came up in the eighth, the Phils had crawled back: They trailed 13-9 with men on first and third. He hit another homer, to pull the Phillies within a run. Remarkably, Philly took a 15-13 lead in the ninth without Schmidt's help, but reliever Tug McGraw botched it, and the game went into extras. In the top of the 10th, Schmidt came up against Paul Reuschel, Rick's brother, and blasted his fourth consecutive home run. This time the lead held up, and the Phillies won, 18-16. Schmidt would overcome the early slump to enjoy one of his finest years, hitting 38 homers and leading the Phillies to a 101-win season.

CARLOS DELGADO
SEPTEMBER 25, 2003

AS THE 2003 SEASON CAME TO A CLOSE, TORONTO'S Carlos Delgado was closing in on two milestones. On the morning of Sept. 25, he woke up needing just one home run to reach the magical 300 plateau for his career, and just one RBI to break his own Blue Jays single-season record of 137. Delgado took care of both marks later that day with one swing of the bat. In the bottom of the first inning, he slammed a three-run homer off Tampa Bay's Jorge Sosa. Delgado didn't stop there, though. He led off the fourth inning with another home run off of Sosa, and then led off the sixth with a third bomb, this time off of lefty Joe Kennedy.

As Delgado stepped to the plate in the eighth with a chance to tie the Major League record of four home runs in a game, he must have chuckled at the circumstances; only 14 players had ever hit four in one game, and the last to do it had been Delgado's best friend and former teammate, Shawn Green, at whose wedding Delgado stood as the best man. Facing the Devil Rays' All-Star reliever Lance Carter, Delgado promptly blasted a changeup over the center-field fence for his fourth homer in four at-bats. "It's the best feeling for a player, doing something against all the odds," Delgado said. "That's what keeps me going." Of the performance, his Manager Carlos Tosca said, "That's the best feat I've ever witnessed on a baseball field."

4-HOME-RUN GAMES

PLAYER	TEAM	DATE
Bobby Lowe	Boston Beaneaters	5/30/1894
Ed Delahanty	Philadelphia Phillies	7/13/1896
Lou Gehrig	New York Yankees	6/3/1932
Chuck Klein	Philadelphia Phillies	7/10/1936
Pat Seerey	Chicago White Sox	7/18/1948
Gil Hodges	Brooklyn Dodgers	8/31/1950
Joe Adcock	Milwaukee Braves	7/31/1954
Rocky Colavito	Cleveland Indians	6/10/1959
Willie Mays	San Francisco Giants	4/30/1961
Mike Schmidt	Philadelphia Phillies	4/17/1976
Bob Horner	Atlanta Braves	7/6/1986
Mark Whiten	St. Louis Cardinals	9/7/1993
Mike Cameron	Seattle Mariners	5/2/2002
Shawn Green	Los Angeles Dodgers	5/23/2002
Carlos Delgado	Toronto Blue Jays	9/25/2003

TATIS'S
HELMET

FERNANDO TATIS
APRIL 23, 1999

UNTIL APRIL 23, 1999, CARDINALS third baseman Fernando Tatis was best known for his wild blond and orange hair. The 24-year-old was a second-generation player who had recently reunited with his father, Fernando Sr., who had left his family in the Dominican Republic to pursue dreams of professional baseball, and stayed in the States. (Tatis Sr. was called to the Majors briefly but never got into a game.)

By 1999, Tatis Jr. had just 19 career homers, but he began the season on a tear, slugging .542 with 11 RBI in his first 14 games, before one crazy night at Dodger Stadium. That evening Tatis hit two grand slams in one *inning*. In the NL's 124 years, only one batter had ever hit two grand slams in one game; Tatis accomplished the feat in one single frame. It's a record that will likely never be broken — and oddly both slams came off one pitcher. As the Cards batted around, Dodgers Manager Davey Johnson left Chan Ho Park in to absorb the beating — and he did, allowing eight hits and 11 runs in 2.2 innings.

"That's what every baseball player is looking for, to be famous," Tatis said. "I think my name is going to be famous." Tatis ended the year with 34 home runs and 107 RBI but, plagued by injury, never played another complete Major League season. Although his career stalled, his achievement does remain famous.

29

HAROLD BAINES MAY 8, 1984

THE WHITE SOX AND BREWERS TOOK THE FIELD ON May 8, 1984, clueless they were beginning a game so long it wouldn't even finish that day. By the time it was over, the teams had played 25 innings over two days, used 15 pitchers and 29 other players, and one team had voluntarily given up its designated hitter. The eight-hour, six-minute marathon was in the books as the Major Leagues' longest game by time.

It was 1-1 after eight innings, and each team scored two in the ninth to send it to extras. Eight scoreless frames followed before the American League implemented its mandatory 1:05 a.m. curfew. The next day things picked up in the 18th. Ben

Oglivie's three-run home run in the 21st seemed certain to send Milwaukee home victorious, but the White Sox clawed back, tying it at 6-6.

The White Sox, however, had pinch-run for their first baseman with pitcher Richard Dotson, who scored the tying run. This left Chicago with no remaining position players, which meant they had to bring their designated hitter, Dave Stegman, in to play the field and their pitchers had to bat. As the game dragged on, the Sox were forced to use Tom Seaver, who was slated to start in the regularly scheduled game later that day. Seaver set the Brewers down 1-2-3 in the top of the 25th. In

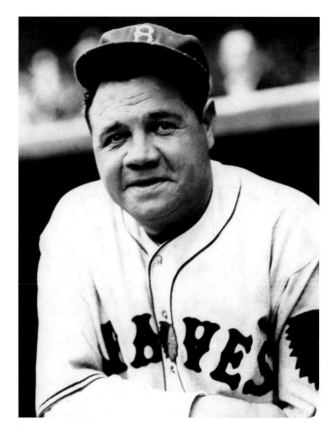

RUTH'S LAST
HOME RUN BALL

the bottom of the inning, the Sox's Harold Baines mercifully ended matters with a walk-off homer off of Milwaukee's Chuck Porter, who was throwing in his eighth inning of relief. The winning pitcher was Seaver, who then took the mound and still pitched 8.1 innings in his scheduled start for his second win of the day.

BABE RUTH MAY 25, 1935

BEFORE THE 1935 SEASON, THE YANKEES CUT TIES with 40-year-old Babe Ruth, who was overweight and had hit "just" 22 home runs in an injury-hampered 1934. Ruth really wanted to manage, so when the Boston Braves offered to bring him back as a player and name him assistant manager, he agreed. It was soon obvious that not only was Ruth finished playing, but the team was not taking him seriously as a manager. They had used him as a gate attraction, and by May, Ruth was batting just below .200 with just three homers.

Aware his career was near its end, Ruth staged a last hurrah versus Pittsburgh on May 25. He hit two-run shots in the first and third innings — the latter off Guy Bush, who heckled Ruth before the famous "Called Shot" in '32. Ruth singled in the fifth, and in the seventh he hit his third home run. A titanic clout, again off Bush, the ball was said to be the longest ever hit at Forbes Field. "I never saw a ball hit so hard before or since," Bush said. "He was fat and old, but he still had that great swing." It's said that Ruth went into the clubhouse and quit on the spot afterward; in truth, it was five days later. But still, the Forbes Field game is remembered as his grand exit.

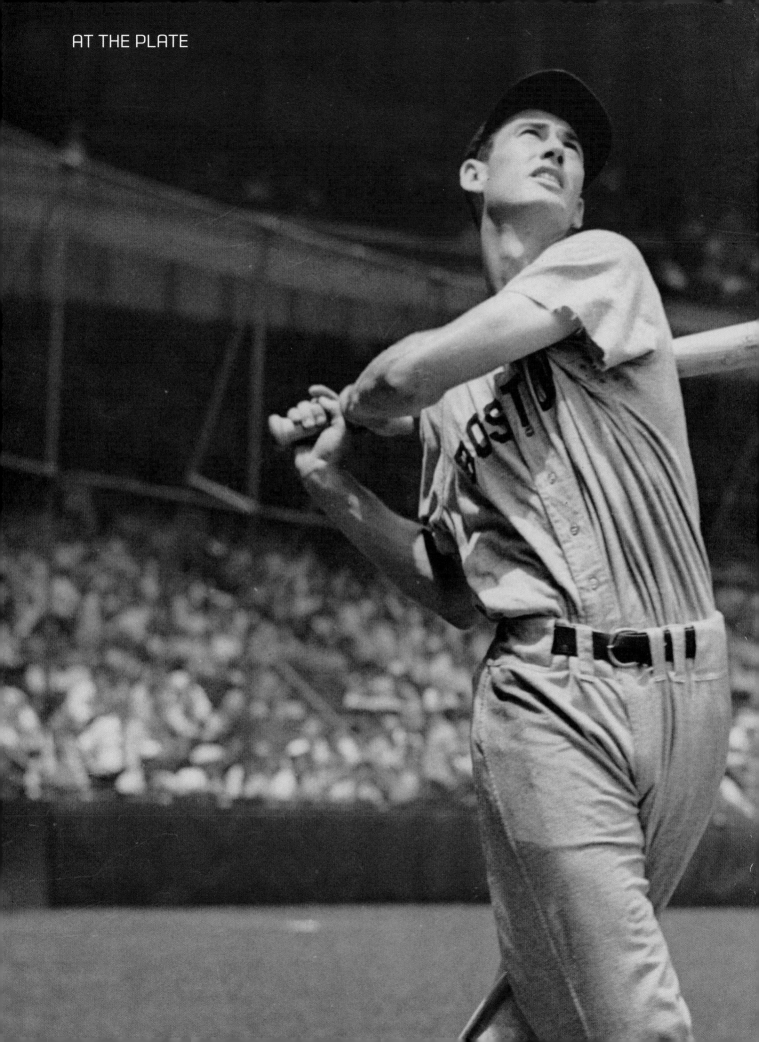

section 2: the hits keep coming

TED WILLIAMS SEPTEMBER 28, 1941

AS THE FABULOUS 1941 SEASON CAME TO AN END, THE QUESTION on everyone's mind was whether Ted Williams could become the first Major Leaguer since 1930 — and the first American Leaguer since 1923 — to hit .400. Williams went 1 for 4 on the second-to-last day of the season, dropping his average from .401 to .39955, which would still have rounded up to .400. Many figured he would sit out the season-ending doubleheader to preserve his average, a common practice. Ty Cobb, for example, had sat out season-ending games in both 1910 and 1911 to preserve his batting title. Williams' teammate Jimmie Foxx had done the same thing in 1938. But Williams was stubborn. "I want to play it out," he told Manager Joe Cronin. "I want to play it all the way." Luckily, Boston's opponent on the last day of the season was the Philadelphia A's, a last-place club whose 4.83 team ERA was easily the worst in the Majors. Manager Connie Mack ordered his hurlers to pitch to Williams as if it were any other game.

Williams wasted no time in sealing the deal. In his first two at-bats, he singled off rookie pitcher Dick Fowler. In his third at-bat, he launched a pitch over the wall for his 37th homer of the season. Williams was now at .404 and would need to go 0 for 5 the rest of the day to fall below the magic threshold. Ignoring the math, Williams just kept on hitting. By the end of the day, he had gone 6 for 8 in the doubleheader, jacked his average up to .406, and earned the respect of fans nationwide for not taking the easy way out. His last hit of the day, a double, would always be remembered by Williams as the hardest ball he ever hit. And although nobody knew it at the time, he had just become the last man to hit .400 in the 20th century.

MARK WHITEN
SEPTEMBER 7, 1993

SEPT. 7, 1993, DIDN'T GET OFF TO A great start for St. Louis outfielder "Hard Hittin'" Mark Whiten. The Cincinnati Reds and Whiten's Cardinals played one of the wildest games in Major League history that day — an exhausting contest that featured 27 runs, 36 hits, six blown leads and a record-tying 15 pitchers used. The Cardinals finally appeared to have things under control with one out in the bottom of the ninth, and a 13-12 lead. But Whiten misplayed a Reggie Sanders fly ball, making it a two-run, walk-off triple. The Cards lost, 14-13.

Fortunately for Whiten, the teams were scheduled for a doubleheader — and what he accomplished in the second game erased everyone's memory of what happened earlier in the day. Whiten caught fire at the plate — more than earning his nickname — and tied Jim Bottomley's long-standing single-game record of 12 RBI. He crushed a grand slam in the first frame, and followed it up with three-run homers in both the sixth and the seventh innings. In the ninth, he came up against Cincinnati's flamethrowing closer Rob Dibble and launched a two-run home run. Aside from tying Bottomley's RBI mark, set in 1924, Whiten also tied the Major League record of four home runs in one game. "I've been around the game 16 years, I've seen some guys do some unbelievable things," teammate Ozzie Smith said, "but nothing like tonight." Said Whiten: "I don't even have words to explain it."

RENNIE STENNETT SEPTEMBER 16, 1975

WHEN THEY MET ON SEPT. 16, 1975, THE CUBS AND Pirates were headed in very different directions. Pittsburgh was cruising toward the National League East title, its fifth crown in six years, while the fifth-place Cubs were playing out the last moments of their third consecutive losing season. The game was over practically as soon as it began, as Chicago starter Rick Reuschel retired just one batter during his time on the mound, allowing eight runs and six hits — two of those to Pittsburgh's leadoff man, Rennie Stennett.

As the Cubs trotted out one mediocre reliever after another, Stennett kept hitting and hitting. By the end of the game, he

had collected a remarkable seven hits in seven at-bats: two doubles, a triple and four singles. No player in the modern era had ever before notched seven hits in a nine-inning game. "You've got to be a good hitter to get seven hits in one game, but you've got to be lucky, too," he admitted. The Panamanian second baseman gave much of the credit for his batting prowess to a late teammate who had served as his hitting mentor. "I think [Roberto] Clemente would be very proud of me," Stennett said. "He told me that even if the pitch is bad, swing at it if you think you can hit it. It's not a bad ball if you get a hit. You can't wait forever for a pitch down the middle."

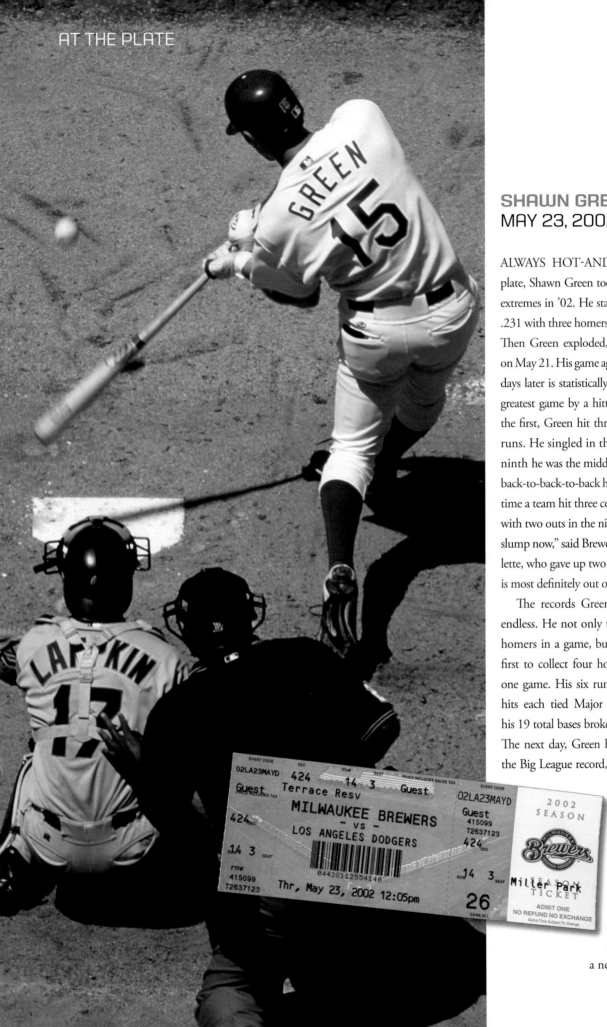

SHAWN GREEN
MAY 23, 2002

ALWAYS HOT-AND-COLD AT THE plate, Shawn Green took streakiness to new extremes in '02. He started off slow, batting .231 with three homers in his first 42 games. Then Green exploded, hitting two homers on May 21. His game against Milwaukee two days later is statistically considered baseball's greatest game by a hitter. After doubling in the first, Green hit three consecutive home runs. He singled in the eighth, and in the ninth he was the middle hitter in a string of back-to-back-to-back homers. It was the first time a team hit three consecutive home runs with two outs in the ninth. "He's out of that slump now," said Brewers pitcher Brian Mallette, who gave up two of Green's shots. "He is most definitely out of that slump."

The records Green set that day seem endless. He not only tied the high of four homers in a game, but he also became the first to collect four homers and six hits in one game. His six runs and five extra-base hits each tied Major League records, and his 19 total bases broke Joe Adcock's record. The next day, Green homered again, tying the Big League record, with five home runs over a two-game span. The day after that, he hit another two shots, giving him a record seven in three games. Add his May 21st game, and Green had nine homers in one week, a new NL record.

MARSHALL McDOUGALL MAY 9, 1999

ALTHOUGH HIS BIG LEAGUE CAREER GOT OFF TO A slow start, Marshall McDougall will be remembered for one of the greatest hitting days in baseball history. While playing second base for Florida State University, he started off a May 9, 1999 game against the Maryland Terrapins modestly enough, smacking a first-inning single. McDougall would then hit home runs in each of his next six at-bats. The outburst included two solo home runs, three three-run shots and a grand slam, as the Florida State Seminoles cruised to a 26-2 lead. "We already had the game in hand so I just kept trying to hit more and improve on my day." After his sixth and final home run, he said, "I was just looking over at the bench. They were going crazy. I was laughing at them because they were as excited as I was."

McDougall's six home runs, 16 RBI and 25 total bases all set new NCAA records. The Jacksonville, Fla. native went on to lead Florida State to that year's College World Series and later became a finalist for the Golden Spikes Award. Although previously considered an iffy draft prospect, McDougall's amazing day propelled him into the ninth round, where he was picked by the Oakland A's. After bouncing around in the Minor Leagues for five years, he finally got called up to The Show by the Texas Rangers in 2005.

chapter 4

INDIVIDUAL PERFORMANCE: ON THE MOUND

In order to comprehend just how impressive a perfect game is, one must understand how rare it is. It's so elusive that most great pitchers in history — Walter Johnson, Lefty Grove, Tom Seaver — never achieved the feat. It's a phenomenon occurring approximately once in every 11,000 Major League games, and as Harvey Haddix can attest, you aren't guaranteed to get your name in the record books even if you successfully navigate nine flawless innings. What Haddix has proven, however, is that perfection isn't required to be absolutely dominant — and sometimes dominant performances are remembered just as fondly as perfect ones.

section 1: perfect games

DON LARSEN OCTOBER 8, 1956

ONE OF YANKEES MANAGER CASEY STENGEL'S QUIRKS was that he liked to keep his pitching staff on its toes. So when hurler Don Larsen showed up at Yankee Stadium for Game 5 of the 1956 World Series, he was in for quite a surprise. "On the Yankees, you never knew if you were pitching until you looked in your locker and discovered that our pitching coach, Jim Turner, had put the ball in your shoe," Bob Turley, one of the team's hurlers, recalled. "So Larsen didn't know he was pitching until he came to the stadium that day."

Larsen had started Game 2 of the Series but struggled to find the plate, walking four and allowing four runs before the Dodgers knocked him out in the second inning. Assuming he wouldn't be relied on after that, Larsen, who allegedly was out late carousing the night before, showed up to the locker room the day of Game 5 exhausted and not ready to take the hill. Told he'd be starting, he trudged to the trainer's room for a pregame nap. After that, a revitalized Larsen threw the game of his life, using an unusual no-windup delivery. He threw 97 pitches, 71 for strikes, handcuffing the Dodgers without once shaking off catcher Yogi Berra. His teammates were on their toes, too, as Mickey Mantle and Gil McDougald robbed Brooklyn batters of hits. With two outs in the ninth, pinch-hitter Dale Mitchell was the only man standing between Larsen and the first perfect game in World Series history. With a 1-2 count, Mitchell was called out on a check swing that remains controversial to this day. The Yanks won the Series in seven, and no pitcher since has come close to duplicating Larsen's feat in the Fall Classic.

LEE RICHMOND
JUNE 12, 1880

BASEBALL HAS GONE THROUGH countless changes over the last 130 years, but nothing has transformed as much as the role of the pitcher. In the 1880s, hurlers threw underhanded from a spot just 45 feet from home plate, the batter requested either a high or a low pitch, and a walk required eight balls. The strain on one's arm was far less than it is today, and pitchers, like other position players, were expected to play nearly every day. In 1880 the left-handed Lee Richmond would pitch 74 of 85 games played by the Worcester Ruby Legs.

With eligibility rules more elastic, Richmond played both collegiate and professional baseball in 1879 and 1880, while attending Brown University. Four days before receiving his medical degree from Brown, Richmond boarded a train bound for Massachusetts to join the Ruby Legs. He went directly from the station to the ballpark, threw on his uniform and proceeded to pitch the first perfect game in the history of professional baseball. Richmond's gem came close to collapsing in the fifth, when Cleveland's Bill Phillips roped an apparent single to the outfield, only for right fielder Lon Knight to save the day by throwing Phillips out at first for a 9-3 groundout. Remarkably, the second-ever perfect game occurred five days later, thrown by Providence's John Ward. Nearly a quarter of a century would pass before anyone pitched another. Richmond would pitch just four more years before leaving baseball to practice medicine.

JIM "CATFISH" HUNTER MAY 8, 1968

OAKLAND FINALLY GOT A MAJOR LEAGUE TEAM IN 1968, and 22-year-old Jim Hunter provided the city's first memorable baseball moment with his performance against the Twins on May 8. The young hurler, known as "Catfish," had already been the Athletics' staff ace since the team's Kansas City days, but joined the game's elite as he threw the first regular-season perfect game in the American League in 46 years. It was only the 11th game played at Oakland Coliseum, and just 6,298 fans dotted the stands.

Throughout the game, A's fielders stayed on their toes, pouncing on any ball hit their way. The turning point came in the seventh, when Hunter went to a 3-2 count on the league's most fearsome slugger, Harmon Killebrew. Instead of throwing the fastball that everyone expected, the young pitcher threw a changeup that Killebrew flailed at, striking out.

In addition to his mastery on the mound, Hunter went 3 for 4 at the plate, driving in three of the game's four runs. In the sixth he broke a scoreless tie with a squeeze bunt so perfect that he actually beat it out for a hit. In the eighth he singled in two insurance runs. Afterward, A's owner Charles O. Finley immediately raised the pitcher's salary by $5,000 — no small amount in those pre-free-agency days.

RANDY JOHNSON
MAY 18, 2004

SINCE RANDY JOHNSON WAS ONE of the greatest pitchers of his generation, it came as no surprise that he hurled some of baseball's most legendary games. He threw a no-hitter in 1990, a three-hitter in a winner-take-all playoff game against the Angels in 1995 and set a record striking out 16 batters in a 2001 relief appearance. Later that year, he earned the win in Game 7 of the World Series for Arizona. But by the time 2004 rolled around, the tall left-hander's record-setting days were believed to be behind him. "I am getting older and less than 100 percent, and a lot of people would be inclined to say, 'He's not going to be the pitcher he was,'" Johnson admitted.

The Atlanta Braves would disagree. On May 18, 2004, Johnson retired 27 straight Braves batters, becoming, at age 40, the oldest pitcher ever to throw a perfect game — surpassing ex-Brave Cy Young's record by three years. "I felt my velocity got better as the game progressed," Johnson said. "My slider was the best it's ever been." His fastball was great, too, reaching 99 mph as he struck out 13 Braves to push his league-leading season total to 81.

The game illustrated Johnson's transformation from a wild young flamethrower into a seasoned vet with pinpoint control. "The no-hitter I threw with Seattle in 1990," he said, "I was far from perfect. I think I walked seven batters. Fourteen years later, I've come a long way. ... My mechanics are not great, but when you're 6-foot-10, there's a lot of room for error. When I was able to gain some consistency in my mechanics, it allowed my ability to take over."

PERFECT GAMES

PLAYER	TEAM	OPPONENT	DATE
Lee Richmond	Worcester	Cleveland Blues	6/12/1880
John Ward	Providence	Buffalo Bisons	6/17/1880
Cy Young	Boston Americans	Philadelphia A's	5/5/1904
Addie Joss	Cleveland Naps	Chicago White Sox	10/2/1908
Charlie Robertson	Chicago White Sox	Detroit Tigers	4/30/1922
Don Larsen	New York Yankees	Brooklyn Dodgers	10/8/1956
Jim Bunning	Philadelphia Phillies	New York Mets	6/21/1964
Sandy Koufax	Los Angeles Dodgers	Chicago Cubs	9/9/1965
Catfish Hunter	Oakland A's	Minnesota Twins	5/8/1968
Len Barker	Cleveland Indians	Toronto Blue Jays	5/15/1981
Mike Witt	California Angels	Texas Rangers	9/30/1984
Tom Browning	Cincinnati Reds	Los Angeles Dodgers	9/16/1988
Dennis Martinez	Montreal Expos	Los Angeles Dodgers	7/28/1991
Kenny Rogers	Texas Rangers	California Angels	7/28/1994
David Wells	New York Yankees	Minnesota Twins	5/17/1998
David Cone	New York Yankees	Montreal Expos	7/18/1999
Randy Johnson	Arizona Diamondbacks	Atlanta Braves	5/18/2004

DAVID CONE JULY 18, 1999

IT WAS YOGI BERRA DAY AT YANKEE STADIUM ON July 18, 1999, and the legendary catcher attended the game along with Don Larsen, the pitcher whom Berra had caught in the first perfect game in Yankees history. Remarkably, the pair witnessed history all over again, as David Cone retired all 27 Montreal Expos to make the Yankees the first franchise ever to pitch three perfect games. (The second had been thrown by David Wells the previous May.)

"I probably have a better chance of winning the lottery than this happening today," Cone gushed to *The New York Times* after his historic feat. "What an honor. All the Yankee legends here. Don Larsen in the park. Yogi Berra Day. It makes you stop and think about the

Yankee magic and the mystique of this ballpark." Counting Larsen's postseason gem, Cone's perfecto was the 16th in Major League history, the first in Interleague Play and just the fifth ever pitched against a team with a designated hitter in the lineup. (The Expos' DH that day was Vladimir Guerrero's older brother, Wilton.)

Under hot, humid conditions — it was 98 degrees and the game was interrupted by a 33-minute rain delay — Cone manhandled Montreal on a mere 88 pitches, aided by outstanding plays from right fielder Paul O'Neill and second baseman Chuck Knoblauch. "This was great," Berra raved afterward. "My day, and Don Larsen's here, this was great. Those pinstripes make you do something."

ERNIE SHORE JUNE 23, 1917

BY 1917, 22-YEAR-OLD BABE RUTH WAS DEVELOPING two different reputations: one as the top left-handed pitcher in baseball, and another as one of the game's most temperamental players. It came as no surprise, then, when on June 23, 1917, Ruth walked the first batter of the game on four pitches and immediately started barking at home plate umpire Brick Owens. In no mood for nonsense, Owens ejected Ruth, who stormed off the mound and punched the ump in the side of the head. Ruth and Owens were separated by the other players before the pitcher departed for the clubhouse; the Bambino would be suspended 10 days and fined $100.

The real story, though, was what happened next. Ernie Shore, a veteran right-hander, came in to pitch for Boston and the runner Ruth had walked was caught stealing. Twenty-six more Washington batters faced Shore and he retired them all — with the help of stellar defense. (Shore struck out just two.) He was hailed as the pitcher of the third perfect game in modern baseball, but years later, a commissioner-appointed committee ruled that it was not a perfect game due to the opening walk. Ruth and Shore are still credited with a combined no-hitter, and nearly a century later, the unusual circumstances make it one of baseball's most legendary games.

HERSHISER'S 1988
WORLD SERIES JERSEY

section 2: domination

OREL HERSHISER   SEPTEMBER 28, 1988

OREL HERSHISER WAS AN OUTSTANDING PITCHER from the moment he made his Major League debut in 1983, but in 1988 the 29-year-old righty went from excellent to otherworldly. It all began on Aug. 30, when Hershiser held the Expos scoreless for the last four innings of a complete-game victory. As September wore on, Hershiser pitched shutout after shutout. His streak stretched to 49 scoreless innings — within striking distance of Don Drysdale's record of 58 frames, long thought to be an absolutely unbreakable mark.

As Hershiser started his last game of the regular season on Sept. 28, he was still nine innings behind Drysdale's record; he could hope only to match the feat. But as fate would have it, the Dodgers and Padres were still scoreless after nine innings, giving Hershiser a chance to pitch the 10th and break the record. As the inning-ending pop fly settled in right fielder Jose Gonzalez's glove, Hershiser knelt in silent prayer. He walked off the mound and Drysdale, who worked as a Dodgers broadcaster and had called the record-breaking game, greeted him with a hug. "I really and truly did not want to break the record," Hershiser told Drysdale. "I wanted to go out and get two outs and walk off and have two Dodgers stay [tied] on top." Replied Big D: "If I had known that, I would have been out there kicking you in the seat of the pants."

Hershiser's dominance continued, and he led Los Angeles to the championship, winning the NLCS and World Series MVP awards. His record during the last two months of the 1988 season reads like a typographical error: 9-0 with a 0.44 ERA over his last 101.3 innings of the season.

SATCHEL PAIGE JULY 4, 1934

IN 1934, 27-YEAR-OLD SATCHEL PAIGE WAS ENJOYING the glorious prime of his lengthy career, beating nearly every team he faced. According to Paige's biographer, Mark Ribowsky, Satchel went 31-4 in 1933 with a streak of 21 straight wins. He got off to a similarly hot start in 1934 and would end up 20-5.

The biggest day of the Negro Leagues season was almost always July 4, when teams played doubleheaders against marquee opponents. In 1934, Pittsburgh's two outstanding Negro Leagues teams, Paige's Pittsburgh Crawfords and the Homestead Grays, faced off at Greenlee Field. Paige dominated the Grays in the first game, striking out eight of the first nine batters on his way to a

no-hitter — one of his three documented no-nos. The Grays were mystified by Paige's heater, which appeared to rise on its way to the plate. Convinced that Paige must be cheating, Buck Leonard, the Grays' slugging first baseman, repeatedly asked the umpire to inspect balls and throw them out. "You may as well throw 'em all out, 'cause they're all gonna jump like that," Paige boasted.

Paige allowed just two base runners — on an error and a walk. The Homestead juggernaut had never been no-hit, and Paige's 17 whiffs matched what was then Dizzy Dean's Major League record. But it was just the start of a hot streak for Paige that included four more shutouts for a total of 45 straight scoreless innings.

48

KERRY WOOD MAY 6, 1998

TALK ABOUT MAKING A FIRST IMPRESSION: IT doesn't get much better than pitching arguably the most dominant game of all time in your fifth Major League start. That's what Kerry Wood did on May 6, 1998, against the Houston Astros. Less than a month after getting called up from Triple-A Iowa, Wood struck out 20, while allowing just one base runner.

Wood threw 122 magnificent pitches that afternoon, reaching triple digits several times. But the key play came in the third, when Ricky Gutierrez hit a slow-rolling grounder that caromed off the heel of third baseman Kevin Orie's mitt for a questionable single — the only base runner Houston would get all day. Wood

tied Roger Clemens' twice-accomplished record for Ks in a nine-inning game, and at age 20 became the first pitcher since Bob Feller to strike out as many batters as his age.

"It's about as well pitched a game as there has been," Cubs President Andy MacPhail said after the game. "An infield hit, no walks, 20 strikeouts, and you had it against the team that is the second-most-prolific scoring team in the National League." Clemens had come nowhere near no-hitters during his 20-K games, and the most strikeouts in a no-hit game is still 16 by Hall of Famer Nolan Ryan. Wood's game, arguably the best ever thrown, was indeed the best of both worlds.

JOHNNY VANDER MEER
JUNE 15, 1938

ON JUNE 15, 1938, FANS POURED into Ebbets Field for what promised to be one of the most exciting baseball games ever played in Brooklyn. It was the first night game in the stadium's history, and festivities included fireworks and a sprinting contest featuring Olympic gold medalist Jesse Owens. If that wasn't enough, hundreds of fans from Midland Park, N.J., were in the house to cheer on their hometown star, Cincinnati Reds pitcher Johnny Vander Meer. The hard-throwing lefty, playing his first full season in the Majors at age 23, had thrown a no-hitter in his previous start. His parents, who were in attendance, presented him with a watch commemorating his accomplishment.

Vander Meer was wild, as he usually was, and although he had walked five batters in the first eight innings, the Dodgers still had not notched a single hit entering the bottom of the ninth. After inducing a leadoff grounder, Vander Meer walked the bases loaded. "What I was doing was forcing my-self, trying to throw the ball harder than I could," he later admitted. Manager Bill McKechnie visited him on the mound and imparted some advice: "Just get it over the plate." Vander Meer did, and the next batter grounded into a force play. With two outs, Dodgers player-manager Leo Durocher was the only man standing between Vander Meer and baseball immortality. Durocher flied out to center, and Vander Meer stood alone as the only pitcher in history ever to pitch consecutive no-hitters. In total, Vander Meer would throw 21.2 hitless innings in a row before giving up a hit in the fourth frame of his next start.

2ND NO-HITTER GAME BALL

BILL FOSTER 1926 PENNANT-DECIDING PLAYOFF, GAMES 8 AND 9

IN 1926, CHICAGO AMERICAN GIANTS LEFTY BILL Foster enjoyed one of the most outstanding pitching seasons in Negro Leagues history, winning 26 consecutive games against varying levels of competition and leading his team to the second-half title in the Negro National League. The American Giants then faced the first-half champs, the Kansas City Monarchs, in a best-of-nine playoff to determine the pennant. The American Giants trailed, 4-games-to-3, prior to Games 8 and 9, which were played as a double-header. In the day's first game, Foster pitched a shutout, out dueling Monarchs' ace Bullet Rogan to tie the series. When Rogan saw Foster warming up to pitch the nightcap, he said: "You pitching?

Then I'm going back, too." In the winner-take-all rematch, Foster pitched his second shutout of the day — a 5-0, darkness-shortened decision that gave his team the pennant.

The American Giants moved on to the best-of-nine Negro League World Series, in which they faced the Bacharach Giants of Atlantic City. Foster gave up 10 hits in the decisive game, but kept his team in a scoreless tie heading to the bottom of the ninth. In that frame, Chicago's Sandy Thompson hit a walk-off single to win both the game and the series for the American Giants. Foster would go on to enjoy a Hall of Fame career, after which he served as a dean at his alma mater, Alcorn State University.

Nomo (left)

HIDEO NOMO
SEPTEMBER 17, 1996

THERE HAVE BEEN MORE THAN 250 no-hitters in Major League history, so it takes more than a mere no-no to get mentioned among the handful of baseball's most legendary pitching performances. But what the Los Angeles Dodgers' Hideo Nomo accomplished on Sept. 17, 1996, ranks as perhaps the most difficult feat achieved by a hurler. After losing a no-hitter in the sixth inning of his previous start, Nomo pitched one against the Colorado Rockies in the high altitude of Coors Field — the most extreme hitters' park in baseball history. And remember, this was before the days of the humidor. In 1996 the park increased offense (a.k.a. its Park Factor) by a whopping 23 percent in comparison to the average Major League stadium. The Rockies had been shut out at Coors Field just twice to that point.

A steady downpour drenched Nomo as he took the hill after a two-hour rain delay. It drizzled throughout the game, and the slippery mound wreaked havoc on Nomo's signature twisting windup. After walking a couple of batters, Nomo ditched the windup in the fourth and pitched from the stretch even when the bases were empty. He bulldozed his way through a Rockies lineup that included the fearsome foursome of Ellis Burks, Dante Bichette, Andres Galarraga and Vinny Castilla, each of whom batted at least .300 with 30 homers and 110 RBI that year. Nomo retired the last 11 hitters in a row, including Burks, who fanned on a late-breaking forkball to end the game. "It's the most incredible thing I've ever seen in baseball," Nomo's teammate Mark Guthrie raved. "You can sit there and say all the superlatives, but people still don't understand what a feat that was."

chapter 5

PITCHERS' DUELS

While home runs are what draw most casual fans to the ballpark, there's nothing a baseball connoisseur enjoys more than a good old-fashioned pitchers' duel. These nail-biting games feature a tension and an artistry thrilling to purists. But there's one group of people that probably doesn't enjoy them so much: the hard-luck losing pitchers. Take the Chicago Cubs' Bob Hendley, for example. On Sept. 9, 1965, not long after getting recalled from the Minors, Hendley pitched the finest game of his career — a complete-game one-hitter — only to lose because his opponent, Hall of Famer Sandy Koufax, pitched a perfect game.

JACK MORRIS VS. JOHN SMOLTZ OCTOBER 27, 1991

APPROPRIATELY FOR A WORLD SERIES MANY believe to be the best of all time, the 1991 Fall Classic had a compelling backstory. No team ever had leapt from last place one season to the World Series the next, but that year *two* teams did it: the Minnesota Twins and Atlanta Braves. With the Series tied, 3-3, after six back-and-forth contests, Game 7 promised an outstanding pitching matchup. Veteran Jack Morris, a St. Paul native, was in his first season for his hometown Twins, while John Smoltz, Atlanta's 24-year-old whippersnapper, was already on his way to becoming baseball's winningest postseason pitcher.

Both hurlers dominated, and for the first time ever, Game 7 of the World Series was tied at zero after nine innings. The Braves blew an excellent chance to score in the eighth when, with Lonnie Smith on first, Terry Pendleton doubled to deep left-center. But Smith was duped by Twins rookie second baseman Chuck Knoblauch, who faked receiving a throw from the outfield to keep Smith from scoring. As zero after zero went up on the scoreboard, Ira Berkow noted in *The New York Times*, "It appeared that the best and concluding moments of this baseball season — maybe the best of any baseball season — might last forever."

Fortunately for the Twins, the game did not last forever. In the bottom of the 10th, Dan Gladden doubled, went to third on a Knoblauch sacrifice and scored the Series-winning run when pinch-hitter Gene Larkin singled over a shallow outfield.

"Every kid has dreamed about this," said Morris, who was named Series MVP after tossing the 10-inning shutout. "When I was a kid, my brother and I used to play Whiffle Ball and I pretended that I was Bob Gibson and he was Mickey Mantle." For one night, at least, Jack Morris was Bob Gibson and then some.

Oeschger

JOE OESCHGER VS. LEON CADORE MAY 1, 1920

IN 1920, TWO PREVIOUSLY UNKNOWN PITCHERS BATTLED IN TWO of the season's most dramatic games; one still stands as the longest pitchers' duel ever. The Braves' Joe Oeschger and Brooklyn's Leon Cadore first faced off on April 20, when Cadore's Robins prevailed — barely — winning, 1-0, in 11 innings.

On Saturday, May 1, Oeschger and Cadore met again. The game sat tied, 1-1, from the sixth on, each pitcher throwing up zero after zero despite close calls. In the ninth, Cadore dodged a bases-loaded jam with a double-play ball, and Oeschger escaped in the 18th when Brooklyn's Ed Konetchy was tagged out at home in the nick of time by Braves catcher Hank Gowdy. "I was just getting tired in the 18th," Oeschger recalled, "but the players kept telling me, 'Just one more inning, Joe … '" Still tied after 26 frames, umpires called the game as darkness descended at 6:50 p.m. Both starters had pitched all 26 innings in just 3 hours, 50 minutes. For the next few days, Oeschger would be forced to brush his teeth left-handed because he couldn't lift his right arm.

FRED TONEY VS. HIPPO VAUGHN
MAY 2, 1917

WRIGLEY FIELD HAS HOSTED many great games, but perhaps none compare to May 2, 1917, when the stadium was still known as Weeghman Park, and Chicago's Hippo Vaughn and Cincinnati's Fred Toney pitched in the closest game to a double no-hitter baseball has ever seen. Vaughn — nicknamed for his 6-foot-4, 240-pound frame — was a wild lefty who frequently walked *and* struck out batters, while Toney was a right-handed spitballer. Regardless, both were backed up plenty that day by their teammates. "Vaughn [was] assisted by remarkable defense by the Chicago infield," one account noted, while another reported, "the Cincinnati outfielders several times saved the game for Toney."

Neither team managed a hit through nine innings. But with one out in the 10th, Reds shortstop Larry Kopf singled to break up Vaughn's no-hitter. Then right fielder Cy Williams dropped a routine fly ball that "any outfielder ordinarily would catch," Vaughn later said. With runners now on second and third, the Reds' Jim Thorpe bounced a swinging bunt back to the mound. Knowing he had little chance to throw out the lightning-quick Thorpe, Vaughn threw home for a play at the plate. But catcher Art Wilson wasn't paying attention, and the ball hit him in the chest protector as the go-ahead run scored. Toney finished off *his* no-hitter in the second half of that inning, but Vaughn's gem would end up in the books as an unofficial no-no.

Toney

Marichal

JUAN MARICHAL VS. WARREN SPAHN   JULY 2, 1963

IT WAS A CHILLY EVENING DURING THE SUMMER OF 1963 when two of baseball's top pitchers, each among the greatest of his generation, thrilled fans at San Francisco's Candlestick Park. Warren Spahn, 42 years old with 338 career wins, sported an 11-3 record on his way to a remarkable 13th 20-win season. His opponent that night was a 25-year-old Juan Marichal, just beginning a great career of his own. He was 12-3 and riding an eight-game winning streak en route to his first 20-win campaign.

The aces kept putting up goose eggs, and both pitched until the scoreless tie entered its 16th inning. "I told [Manager Al] Dark in the 15th, 'I'm not leaving while that old guy is still on the mound,'"

Marichal recalled. "I didn't want that old man lasting longer than me. But he was incredible, and I wound up staying there a lot longer than I thought I would." Both teams missed chances to score. Spahn, an excellent hitting pitcher, doubled in the seventh but was stranded. In the 14th, the Giants loaded the bases, but Spahn wriggled free. Finally, at 12:31 a.m., Willie Mays tagged Spahn for a walk-off homer, ending one of history's great pitching duels. It was a tough loss for the crafty Spahn, who had lasted 15.1 innings mostly on guile, striking out just two batters. "It was supposed to be a screwball, but it didn't do anything but float," Spahn told historian Mike Attiyeh. "It didn't break like I wanted. It didn't break at all."

Haddix

LEW BURDETTE VS. HARVEY HADDIX
MAY 26, 1959

HARVEY HADDIX WOKE UP IN A Milwaukee hotel on May 26, 1959, with a cough and a sore throat. Little did he know, later he would hurl one of baseball's finest games. The 33-year-old lefty would face the defending-NL-champ Braves and their ace, Lew Burdette. Haddix didn't allow a Milwaukee base runner through nine innings, and threw just 78 pitches. Burdette was almost as good, holding Pittsburgh scoreless in response. Haddix pitched 12 perfect frames. "[He] was just methodical," Burdette told historian Danny Peary. Even though he fanned just eight, Haddix carved Milwaukee up with curveballs, forcing weak grounders and flies.

But Haddix's perfecto crumbled in the 13th, when third baseman Don Hoak bounced a throw that first baseman Rocky Nelson could not pick. Eddie Mathews sacrificed, and Haddix walked Hank Aaron to face Joe Adcock, who collected the Braves' first hit — a walk-off home run making Haddix one of history's hardest-luck losers. But the hit was odd, as County Stadium had two fences; one lined the outfield and the other stood behind it. Aaron "saw the ball hit a fence and thought it was the front fence and assumed the ball was still in play," Burdette said. Thinking the winning run had scored, Aaron peeled off toward the dugout. Adcock was called out for passing him on the bases. The official score went from 3-0 to 1-0. "All I know is that we lost," Haddix said. "What's so historic about that?"

Williams

Joss (left), Walsh

SMOKEY JOE WILLIAMS VS. CHET BREWER AUGUST 2, 1930

LOOKING FOR WAYS TO DRAW FANS AS THE GREAT Depression began to haunt America in 1930, the Kansas City Monarchs of the Negro Leagues began playing at night. Five years later, Cincinnati would become the first Major League team to install lights. But the Monarchs had first pioneered a floodlight system that they hauled around on 12 trucks. By August, they had toured their invention to many cities, and returned home to face another Negro Leagues powerhouse, the Homestead Grays.

The game featured Chet Brewer, the Monarchs' 23-year-old flamethrower, against the Grays' Smokey Joe Williams, who, at 44, was nearing the end of a brilliant career. Both pitchers reportedly specialized in doctoring baseballs, which wasn't explicitly banned in the Negro Leagues. A combination of primitive lighting and late-breaking pitches rendered it nearly impossible for anyone to get a hit. The game was scoreless entering the 12th inning, when Chaney White hit a liner off of third base, allowing Oscar Charleston to score the go-ahead run. Williams completed his masterpiece in the bottom of the inning, finishing with a one-hit shutout with 27 strikeouts. Brewer, the *loser*, struck out 19 batters — 10 of them in a row.

ADDIE JOSS VS. ED WALSH OCTOBER 2, 1908

TWO OF BASEBALL'S GREATEST PITCHERS WENT toe-to-toe for the AL pennant on Oct. 2, 1908. As Chicago's White Sox and Cleveland's Naps took the field, both teams trailed first-place Detroit; the Naps by half a game and the Sox by a game and a half. Each team sent its ace to the hill. Cleveland's Addie Joss, with impeccable control, would finish the year 24-11, with a then-league-record 1.16 ERA. Meanwhile, Chicago spitballer Ed Walsh would go a record-breaking 40-15, with a 1.42 ERA.

A brilliant Walsh struck out 15 and allowed just four hits. But in the third, Cleveland scored when Chicago catcher Ossee Schreckengost let a pitch get away for a passed ball. Cleveland's Joss, meanwhile, had yet to allow a base runner. Late in the game, fans watched in nervous silence. "A mouse working his way along the grandstand floor," one writer noted, "would have sounded like a shovel scraping over concrete." With two outs in the ninth, Chicago's John Anderson hit an apparent double down the line, which landed foul. Given another chance, Joss forced a grounder to third baseman Bill Bradley, who bobbled it but threw in time to retire Anderson for the final out. Perfect game or no, the Naps finished half a game behind Detroit in the pennant race.

SMOKY JOE WOOD VS. WALTER JOHNSON
SEPTEMBER 6, 1912

AS THE 1912 SEASON ENTERED ITS dog days, Boston's Smoky Joe Wood and Washington's Walter Johnson were in the midst of impressive winning streaks. In fact, both had spent much of the season battling for the title of baseball's best pitcher. In response to one reporter's query, the veteran Johnson said, "Can I throw harder than Joe Wood? Listen, my friend, there's no man alive who can throw harder than Smoky Joe Wood." The 22-year-old Wood, for his part, opined that "the greatest pitcher who ever lived was Walter Johnson."

Johnson's winning streak had been snapped at an amazing 16 victories — an AL record prior to this matchup. By September, Wood had gained on him, winning 13 in a row. With the Senators scheduled to visit Boston, the teams agreed to move Wood's start up a day so Johnson would have the chance to defend his record. The frantically hyped Fenway matchup was pure madness. Many in the overflowing crowd stood on the field, filling up all of foul territory and much of the outfield. "I never saw so many people in one place in my life," Wood said. "It was so crowded down there I hardly had time to warm up." The game, almost inevitably, ended up 1-0, in Wood's favor. The lone run scored when two consecutive Red Sox fly balls, normally routine plays, landed in the roped-off crowd for ground-rule doubles. Wood would win two more games to tie Johnson before losing. To this day, the two remain co-record holders.

Wood (left), Johnson

chapter 6
BIZARRE PLAYS

Although there has never been a shortage of dramatic baseball moments, the comical or controversial interludes are often the most memorable. Few who were there will ever forget the Minor League game in which Rodney McCray ran through the outfield wall trying to make a catch. Or the game in which Pirates Manager Lloyd McClendon literally stole first base, storming off with the bag after being ejected. Some moments remain mysterious even years later. Nobody knows exactly why, during a 1971 game, a sack of flour fell from the sky onto Dodger Stadium's infield. All we know is that the infielders finished the game with flour on their faces.

THE PINE TAR GAME   JULY 24, 1983

IN 1983 THERE WERE FEW FIERCER RIVALS IN BASEBALL THAN THE Yankees and Royals, who had met in the ALCS in four of the previous seven years. So when the teams squared off at Yankee Stadium on July 24, it was a hotly contested showdown in a playoff-type atmosphere. With the Yankees ahead, 4-3, and two outs in the ninth inning, Manager Billy Martin brought in closer Goose Gossage to face George Brett. The star third baseman won the showdown of future Hall of Famers, smacking a two-run homer to give Kansas City the lead. But Martin had a trick up his sleeve. Earlier in the year, he had noticed that Brett liked to slather his bat with pine tar — enough that it violated an obscure rule banning application of any substance more than 18 inches above the bat's knob. Having saved this ammunition, Martin pounced, immediately protesting that Brett's homer be disallowed. With no tape measure on hand, the umpires used 17-inch-wide home plate to approximate a measurement. After much discussion, ump Tim McClelland ruled Brett out, giving the Yankees an immediate victory. A wild-eyed Brett charged out of the dugout and had to be restrained from attacking McClelland, who then ejected him from a game that was already over.

Not surprisingly, Kansas City protested the call. The Royals' objection was upheld by AL President Lee MacPhail, who noted that while the rule book prohibited excessive pine tar use, nowhere did it offer a repercussion. Brett's homer was reinstated, and the game was resumed from that point on Aug. 18. In the replay, Martin staged a protest of his own, making a mockery of the proceedings by playing pitcher Ron Guidry in center field and left-handed first baseman Don Mattingly at second base. The Yanks made three uneventful outs in the bottom of the ninth, and Kansas City claimed its overdue 5-4 victory.

Hartnett (center)
mobbed after
homering the
Cubs to first
place in 1938

GABY HARTNETT
SEPTEMBER 28, 1938

AT THE START OF SEPTEMBER 1938, the Chicago Cubs were mired in third place, seven games behind league-leading Pittsburgh. But the Cubbies got hot, going 22-7 that month under the leadership of veteran catcher Gabby Hartnett, who had been named player-manager in July. By the time the Cubs and Pirates faced off at Wrigley Field on Sept. 28, Chicago was within half a game; a victory would propel the Cubs into first place, with just five games left to play in the regular season.

It was a see-saw contest, with Pittsburgh taking leads of 3-1 and 5-3, only for the Cubs to tie it up each time. As dusk settled on Wrigley Field, the game entered the ninth tied, 5-5. The umpires agreed it would be the last inning before the game would be called due to darkness. (Wrigley wouldn't get lights until 1988.) After the Pirates bowed out meekly in the top half of the frame, the first two Cubs batters went down, too. That brought up Hartnett. Firing fastballs in the dim light, Pirates pitcher Mace Brown quickly got Hartnett in an 0-2 hole. But to the disbelief of all, Hartnett sent the next pitch into the left-field bleachers for a walk-off homer. It was so dark that Hartnett could barely see the bases as he jogged to touch each one. The "Homer in the Gloamin'" and the Cubs victory "are the two greatest things that ever happened to me," Hartnett said. Another happened three days later: The Cubs clinched the pennant.

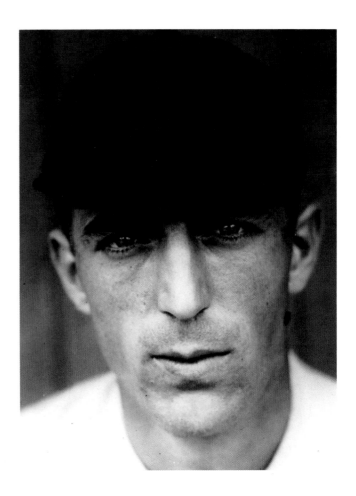

FRED MERKLE
SEPTEMBER 23, 1908

IN 1908 THE CUBS, GIANTS AND PIRATES ALL BATTLED for a World Series berth, resulting in one of baseball's greatest pennant races. On Sept. 23, the Giants hosted the Cubs in a thrilling game. Tied, 1-1, in the bottom of the ninth with two outs and a man on first, Giants rookie Fred Merkle scratched out a hit. Al Bridwell followed with an apparent game-winning single. As the crowd stormed the field, players dashed to the clubhouses. This included Merkle, who ran only about 15 feet toward second base before heading to the clubhouse for safety.

Cubs second baseman Johnny Evers realized that Merkle never touched second base, and could still be retired on a force play. With fans gallivanting around him, Evers waved for the ball, but Giants coach Joe McGinnity intercepted the throw and hurled the ball deep into the stands. Evers simply got another, and making sure umpire Hank O'Day was watching, stepped on second base. The winning run was revoked, and the game remained an official tie to be replayed at the end of the season, if necessary. Of course, it became necessary, and the Giants lost, giving the pennant to the Cubs — and ensuring a place for poor Fred Merkle in the pantheon of baseball boneheads.

EDDIE GAEDEL
AUGUST 19, 1951

AFTER BUYING THE MINOR League Milwaukee Brewers in 1941, Bill Veeck became known as baseball's most inventive and unpredictable owner. Despite this reputation, nobody was prepared for the epic stunt the St. Louis Browns owner pulled on Aug. 19, 1951: signing midget Eddie Gaedel and sending him up to bat against the Detroit Tigers. Veeck scrupulously made sure everything was by the book. He couldn't be blamed, after all, if the league office failed to inquire about the height of the new player he had signed or the unfamiliar name listed on the scorecard with the uniform number 1/8.

When sent up to pinch-hit, the 3-foot-7 Gaedel never took his miniature bat off his shoulder. He walked on four pitches as laughing Detroit pitcher Bob Cain failed to find Gaedel's tiny strike zone.

Although Cain and his teammates may have been amused, the prank did not please AL President Will Harridge, who immediately banned Gaedel and ruled that from then on, all new player signings were subject to prior approval by the league. In response, Veeck questioned Phil Rizzuto, the Yankees' diminutive shortstop. "I was going to demand an official ruling on whether he was a short ballplayer or a tall midget," Veeck said. Of course, Harridge prevailed. Once again, Veeck had fought the law and the law had won. But one thing nobody could ever take away from Eddie Gaedel was the Major League record for highest career on-base percentage.

Maier

YANKEES VS. ORIOLES   OCTOBER 9, 1996

THE ORIOLES WERE LEADING THE YANKEES, 4-3, in the eighth inning of Game 1 of the ALCS when New York's rookie shortstop, Derek Jeter, flied deep to right. Orioles right fielder Tony Tarasco calmly glided back toward the wall, but just as he was about to catch the ball, a glove jutted out and deflected it into the stands. The glove belonged to 12-year-old Little Leaguer Jeffrey Maier, who was standing in the aisle just behind the right-field wall. Despite the Orioles' heated protests, umpire Rich Garcia ruled (incorrectly, replays showed) that Maier had not interfered with Tarasco because the ball was already in the stands. Thanks to the gift provided by Maier, Jeter's homer tied the game. The Yanks won the contest in the 11th, and eventually took the pennant. Orioles fans were enraged, not only at the illegitimate home run, but also at the way the mischievous youngster was applauded for breaking the rules. Maier was feted on national talk shows and provided with a luxury limo by the New York *Daily News*. Said Yankees Manager Joe Torre: "I think it's glorifying the wrong thing." Maybe so, but Jeffrey Maier will always be remembered as a hero in the Bronx.

MARLINS VS. CUBS
OCTOBER 14, 2003

THE LONG-SUFFERING CUBS LED THE UP-start Marlins, 3-0, entering the eighth inning of the NLCS Game 6 — a comfortable enough lead with their ace, Mark Prior, on the mound at Wrigley Field. Prior allowed a double before forcing a Luis Castillo pop-up in foul territory. The Cubs' Moises Alou reached into the stands along the left-field line to snag it, but was foiled when a head-phones-wearing Cubs fan, Steve Bartman, went for the ball. Alou angrily complained, but the umpires correctly ruled that there was no interference. Bartman had every right to go for the ball, because even though Alou had a play on it, the ball was in the stands. Castillo eventually walked, and Prior proceeded to completely self-destruct, aided by a key error from shortstop Alex Gonzalez. The Marlins went on to win both the game and, the next night, the series. Although some tried to compare the Bartman incident with the antics of Jeffrey Maier, the situations were very different: Bartman did not break the rules, and it was only one part of a much larger collapse at the end of the game. Florida needed just four runs to take the lead — the Cubs allowed them eight.

Bartman

chapter 7

RIVALS

Baseball has some of sports' most storied rivalries. Over the decades, these feuds have become a part of the national consciousness. They are as hotly contested as any clash between the Hatfields and the McCoys or the Montagues and the Capulets ever was. Although Yankees-Red Sox has blazed brighter recently, the best rivalry over time has been between the Dodgers and Giants, playing out on two coasts for nearly 120 years. One sure sign of a healthy rivalry is when one team takes pleasure simply in causing the other pain.

RED SOX VS. YANKEES
OCTOBER 17, 2004

AS MARIANO RIVERA STARED DOWN KEVIN MILLAR on Oct. 17, 2004, all of Red Sox Nation felt the crushing weight of the Curse of the Bambino. The Sox had enjoyed a fantastic 98-win season, and yet here they were in Game 4 of the ALCS, about to be swept out of the postseason by the Yankees. As if being down 3-games-to-none in the series and 4-3 in the game weren't enough, they were up against Rivera, arguably the best pitcher in postseason history. But Millar walked to lead off the ninth, giving the Sox a sliver of hope, however small.

Enter Dave Roberts. Picked up from the Dodgers in a deadline trade, the master thief had been acquired for one strategic purpose: to pinch-run when the Sox needed a stolen base. Everybody in the park knew Roberts was going to steal second. He got the base anyway, sliding in safely despite an on-the-money throw from Jorge Posada. "I was scared, excited," Roberts told the *Boston Globe*. "I can't tell you how many emotions went through me." Bill Mueller singled to drive in Roberts and tie the game. The Red Sox ultimately won in 12 innings on a towering home run by David Ortiz.

With fate now clearly on their side, the Sox didn't lose again. They became the first team ever to overcome a three-game deficit to win a seven-game series. Then they swept the Cardinals in the World Series to bury the Curse once and for all. And it was all made possible by a single stolen base. "As long as baseball is played in Boston," the *Globe*'s Bob Ryan wrote, "Dave Roberts will be remembered."

GIANTS VS. DODGERS OCTOBER 3, 1951

BY THE MORNING OF AUG. 12, 1951, THE NEW York Giants had pretty much lost hope. They had just dropped four games in a row and sunk 13 games behind their rivals, the first-place Brooklyn Dodgers. Not even a perfected sign-stealing system — in which a bench player hid in the Polo Grounds' center-field clubhouse with a telescope, picked up signs and relayed them to the dugout via an electronic buzzer — seemed to help. But beginning with that day's doubleheader, the Giants embarked on a 16-game winning streak that would end up catapulting them back into the pennant race. By the end of the season they were tied with the Dodgers, forcing a three-game playoff for the National League pennant.

It all came down to the third game, which the Dodgers led, 4-1, in the ninth. But Brooklyn starter Don Newcombe gave up three hits, bringing up Bobby Thomson as the potential winning run. Brooklyn Manager Charlie Dressen had two pitchers warming up, and chose to put in Ralph Branca after Carl Erskine threw a warm-up curve in the dirt. It was a chance at redemption for Branca, who, two days earlier, had given up what became the game-ending homer to Thomson. But Thomson hit him again, pulling a ball into the bleachers for a homer dubbed "The Shot Heard 'Round the World." As Thomson rounded the bases, Giants announcer Russ Hodges famously screamed: "The Giants win the pennant! The Giants win the pennant!"

DiMaggio

YANKEES VS. RED SOX
JUNE 29, 1949

THE YANKEES SPENT THE EARLY part of 1949 barely hanging on to first place while their star, Joe DiMaggio, sat out the season's first 65 games with a bone spur in his foot. On June 28, with the Yanks just five games ahead of the pesky Sox, the teams played at Fenway Park. DiMaggio, determined to get back on the field, took so much batting practice before the series that his hands started to bleed, but he didn't care. "There's no pain in my foot," he said. "That's what matters." In his first at-bat in more than two months, DiMaggio knocked a single. In his second at-bat he slammed the ball over the wall, and the Yankees won the first game, 5-4.

By the second game of the weekend set, the nation was captivated by the news that Joe DiMaggio was back. In the fifth, he homered over the Green Monster. He came up in the eighth with the score tied, and Sox reliever Earl Johnson threw what he thought was the perfect ball — a low, inside curveball that it seemed not even DiMaggio could hit fair. But somehow he did, launching another homer over the Monster. It proved to be the game-winner, and afterward, when asked if his foot was still hurting, DiMaggio replied, "Nothing hurts when you play like this." Led by DiMaggio, the Yanks eventually held off Boston to win the pennant by one game.

YANKEES VS. RED SOX OCTOBER 16, 2003

UNTIL THE FINAL MOMENT OF THE ALCS, 2003 HAD been a disaster for Yanks third baseman Aaron Boone, who displayed what *New York Times* writer Bruce Weber called an "invisibility in the batter's box." In 31 postseason at-bats, Boone had hit .161 with no extra-base hits. His slump was so bad that he was replaced in Game 7 by utility infielder Enrique Wilson, who entered the game a .253 hitter, but who had had more success against Pedro Martinez, Boston's starting pitcher that day. But Martinez, after talking Manager Grady Little into leaving him on the mound, imploded in the eighth as the Yankees rallied to tie the game. Boone entered that fateful inning as a pinch-runner but was stranded on second.

Since the Yankees had pinch-hit for Wilson, they had little choice but to leave Boone in to play third base. Almost by default, he remained in the lineup as the game entered extra innings tied at 5-5.

The Sox prepared for the long haul by sending durable knuckle-baller Tim Wakefield, a starter, to the mound in the 10th. He shut the Yankees down that inning, but would return in the 11th to throw just one pitch — a hanging knuckleball — which Boone drove down the left-field line for a series-winning homer. Dancing around the bases, his 5-for-31 start was forgotten. "It took a while, but I showed up," he said. His brother Bret, a Big Leaguer himself, added: "You get a big hit, everyone forgets about the bad at-bats."

77

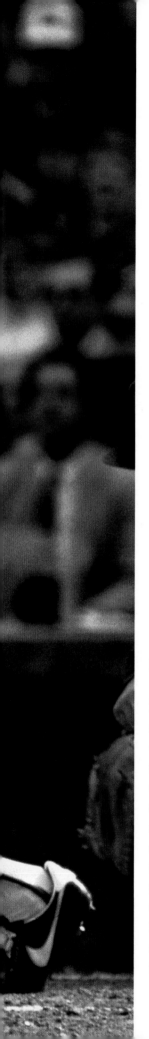

CUBS VS. CARDINALS JUNE 23, 1984

IN 1984 THE CUBS, WHO HAD FINISHED LAST or next-to-last in the five previous seasons, surprised all with a 36-31 start. On June 23, the team faced its first test of the season against the rival Cardinals in a nationally televised game at Wrigley. It would not only be one of the most memorable games in Cubs regular-season history, but also a milestone for young second baseman Ryne Sandberg. The Cards quickly took a 9-3 lead, but Chicago answered, scoring five in the sixth inning to make it 9-8. In the ninth, Sandberg (already 3 for 4) came up against Hall of Fame closer Bruce Sutter with a chance to tie it up. He did the next-to-impossible, lofting a game-tying homer — just the fourth longball Sutter had allowed all year.

But the Cardinals scored twice in the 10th when Willie McGee doubled to complete the cycle. Not to be topped, Sandberg came up in the bottom of the 10th and hit *another* game-tying shot off Sutter. Although Dave Owen's pinch-hit single won it for the Cubs in 11, it was Sandberg's 5-for-6, seven-RBI day that we talk about. "Sandberg is the best player I have ever seen," Cards Manager Whitey Herzog said.

"I was almost in a fog after the game," Sandberg told the *Chicago Tribune*. "That game really propelled the team." The Cubs reached the playoffs for the first time in 39 years, and Sandberg would be voted NL MVP. Even more than 20 years later, Sandberg says, "Everyone tells me where they were when they watched that game."

79

Dent (center)

YANKEES VS. RED SOX
OCTOBER 2, 1978

BOSTON RED SOX FANS WERE convinced that 1978 was going to be the year that their heartbreak would come to an end. Boasting the best hitter in the American League, Jim Rice, Boston bolted strong out of the gate and in late July led the fourth-place Yankees by 14 games. These being the Red Sox, however, things got complicated. New York, thanks to unbelievable pitching from lefty Ron Guidry, crept back into the race and found itself tied for first on Sept. 10. The two teams exchanged blows after that, finishing the season still tied for first place. The division title would come down to a one-game playoff on Oct. 2 at Boston's Fenway Park.

Guidry, 24-3 on the year, took on Mike Torrez. Surprisingly, Torrez pitched shut-out baseball, while Guidry allowed the Sox to take a 2-0 lead. But it all changed in the seventh when light-hitting Yankees shortstop Bucky Dent came up with two runners on and two outs. Dent had hit just 22 home runs in his five-year career, but he launched a Torrez pitch over the famed Green Monster in left field for a go-ahead, three-run homer. "I've been struggling and I can't believe it, really," Dent said. "It was the biggest hit of my career." Guidry and the Yankees held on to win the game, the AL East title, and eventually the World Series. Sox fans, meanwhile, coined a new (and unprintable) nickname for Dent.

GIANTS VS. DODGERS OCTOBER 3, 1962

ON PAPER, THE 1962 DODGERS SEEMED unbeatable. They had NL MVP Maury Wills, Cy Young winner Don Drysdale and outfielder Tommy Davis, winner of that year's batting (.346) and RBI (153) titles. As if that wasn't enough, Sandy Koufax was the NL ERA champ. All that talent made taking the National League seem like a piece of cake — but games aren't played on paper. On Sept. 23, the Dodgers had a four-game lead with just seven left to play, but they dropped six and allowed the Giants to tie, setting up a repeat of 1951 — a three-game playoff for the NL pennant.

Koufax, fresh off a finger injury that shelved him for two months, was crushed, 8-0, in the first game. The next day, the Giants knocked Drysdale out in the top of the

sixth, only to get stunned themselves when the Dodgers scored seven in the bottom of the inning. Los Angeles later won in the bottom of the ninth when Wills scored on a sac fly, tying the series. Everything came down to Game 3 at Dodger Stadium on Oct. 3 — 11 years to the day after Bobby Thomson's 1951 heroics. Los Angeles again led, 4-2, entering the ninth. And again, the Giants mounted a furious rally. Dodgers pitchers Stan Williams, Ed Roebuck and Ron Perranoski couldn't find the plate, combining for five walks and a wild pitch, as the Giants came from behind to win the flag. "I wouldn't say this matches our playoff victory of 1951," statesman Willie Mays admitted. "It wasn't as dramatic. ... [But] it means a lot more to these young fellows."

Saltalamacchia
(center)

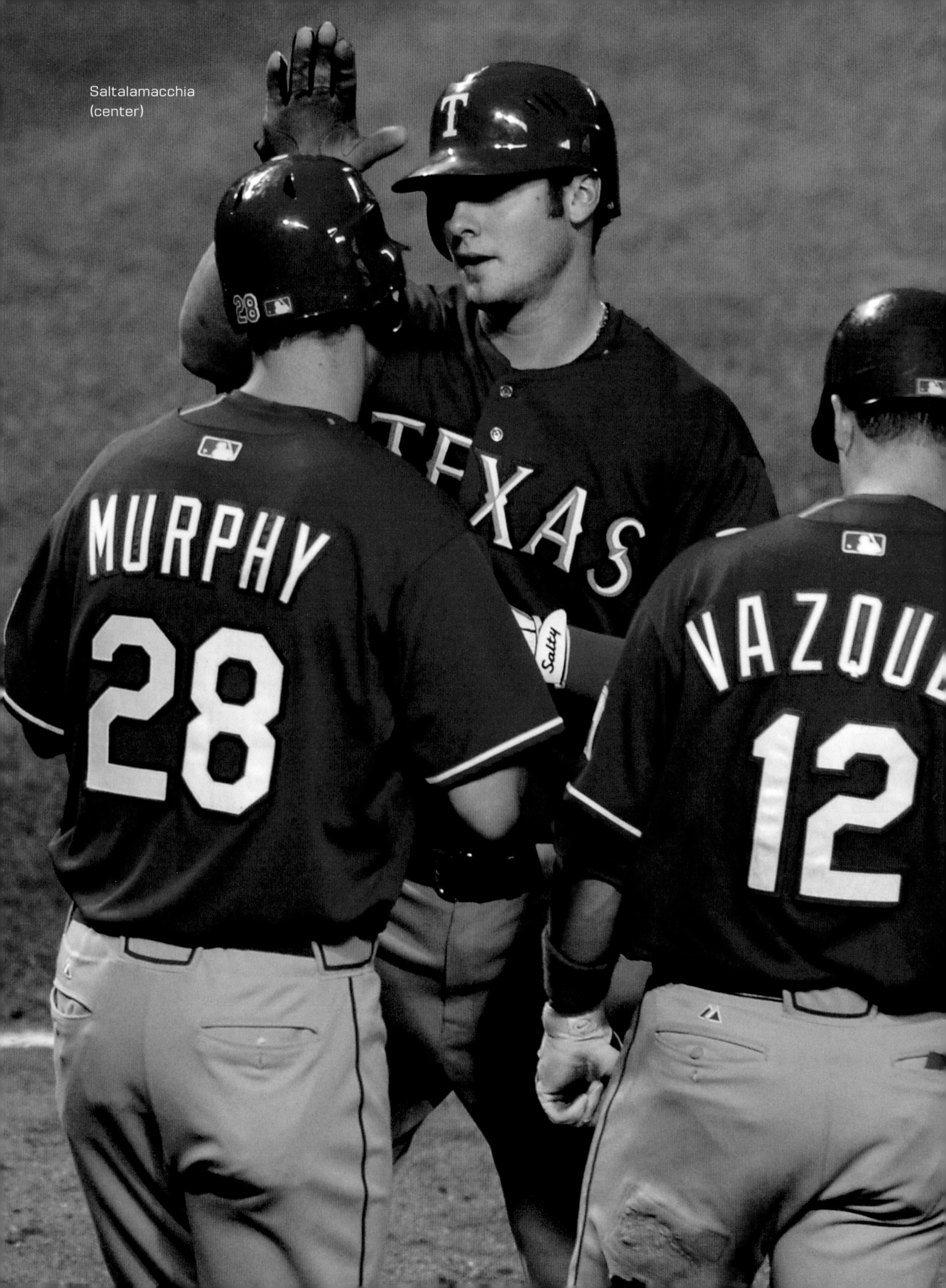

chapter 8

TEAM PERFORMANCE: OFFENSE

Ballplayers tend to talk about hitting as if it's a contagion, something that can be passed from batter to batter like a cold. "It's fun when everyone's involved and everybody's swinging the bat well," Houston's Josh Anderson said in 2007 after his Astros blew out the Cardinals, 18-1. "This is special, to be part of something like this." Indeed, some of the most memorable games, for both fans and players, are the ones in which the hits come in bunches — and keep coming.

TEXAS RANGERS AUGUST 22, 2007

AUGUST 2007 WAS A TRYING TIME FOR THE Texas Rangers, who were struggling to score. That month they ranked 11th in the AL in runs and 12th in batting average and scored just three runs a game — until they played a doubleheader at Baltimore on Aug. 22. In the first game, their hitting frustration came pouring out, and by the time the carnage was over, Texas had clobbered the Orioles, 30-3. It was the most runs ever scored by an AL team and the most by any Big League club since 1897. "I knew we'd get the bats going, but I never expected anything like this," Rangers Manager Ron Washington said. "When the faucet is on, you want it to stay on. You never want to cut it off."

Jarrod Saltalamacchia and Ramon Vazquez led the charge, both with two homers and seven RBI. They were supported by some unlikely performances from David Murphy, playing in just his eighth game with Texas after being acquired from Boston, and third baseman Travis Metcalf, called up from Triple-A that morning. Murphy collected five hits and scored five runs, while Metcalf entered in the seventh, hit a grand slam and scored twice. "It was awesome in capital letters," Metcalf said. But not for Baltimore, whose team ERA jumped from seventh to 11th place in the AL (hitting 4.60 after the game), or for Paul Shuey, whose own ERA leapt from 6.75 to 9.49.

Anson

CHICAGO COLTS
JUNE 29, 1897

ALTHOUGH THE BIRTH OF THE home run era was still many years away, the 1890s were a time of prosperity for anyone who held a bat in his hands. Thanks to poorly groomed playing fields, pocketless fielders' gloves and the fact that foul balls did not yet count as strikes, runs were scored at record levels during the decade. In 1897, for instance, the average National League team piled up nearly six runs and more than 10 hits per game. Things reached a head on June 29 of that year, when Chicago Colts batters enjoyed what *The New York Times* called "the greatest picnic of the season" — or, for that matter, of any season.

Led by player-manager Cap Anson, who was playing in his 27th and final season, the Colts (who would become known as the Cubs in 1903) beat the Louisville Colonels that afternoon, 36-7, setting a single-game scoring record that still stands today. The run total was more than the Colts, mired in 11th place, had scored in the previous eight games combined. Colonels starter Chick Fraser gave up a brutal 14 runs in 2.1 innings, but it was Jim Jones who absorbed the worst of the beating. Jones, a rookie outfielder who had yet to play in a game, was called on to make his debut as a mop-up pitcher. He coughed up 22 runs — although just 14 of them were earned — over 6.2 innings. After his rough debut, Jones would make just one more appearance for Louisville before being sent back down to the minors. He wouldn't see a Big League field again until 1901.

Bell

TORONTO BLUE JAYS SEPTEMBER 14, 1987

AFTER MUCH OF THE 1980s WAS DOMINATED BY pitching, things took a dramatic turn in 1987 as home runs jumped a whopping 17 percent — from 3,813 to 4,458. Even a singles hitter like Wade Boggs was able to stroke 24, tripling his previous season high. A number of hitting feats were accomplished during the season, but none as shocking as the one pulled off by Toronto on Sept. 14.

The Jays, in a dogfight with the Tigers for the AL East title, smashed 10 homers (a new Big League record) on their way to bludgeoning Baltimore, 18-3. Those going deep included center fielder Lloyd Moseby and rookies Fred McGriff and Rob Ducey. Rance Mulliniks and soon-to-be AL MVP George Bell knocked two home

runs each, and catcher Ernie Whitt became the second Blue Jay ever to hit three in one game. With the game out of hand in the eighth, the O's decided to pull Cal Ripken Jr., resting him for the first time in five-and-a-half years and ending his record streak of 8,243 straight innings played. Unfortunately for Cal, the manager who made the decision was also a man he couldn't argue with — Cal Ripken Sr.

Sadly for Toronto fans, the game would prove to be the last highlight of the Blue Jays' once-promising season. They entered the final week with a three-and-a-half-game lead over Detroit, but would drop each of their last seven contests to hand the division crown to the Tigers.

LOS ANGELES DODGERS SEPTEMBER 18, 2006

WITH THE DODGERS AND PADRES IN A GRIPPING pennant race, fans at Dodger Stadium on Sept. 18, 2006, figured they were in for a good game. What they witnessed was one of the most dramatic and tense regular-season contests in decades. By the time it was over, they'd seen a near-fight, two separate comebacks from four-run deficits, a blown save by a future Hall of Famer, a home run record likely never to be broken and a come-from-behind,

walk-off homer. "If you were a non-biased baseball fan, it was one of the greatest games you ever watched," Dodgers pitcher Derek Lowe said. "Nobody in this room can describe anything that happened."

The Padres plated four runs in the first, but the Dodgers chipped away, tying it up at the end of three. L.A. entered the ninth trailing by one, but closer Takashi Saito gave up three runs to make it 9-5 San Diego. Jeff Kent homered to start the ninth, but Dodgers fans

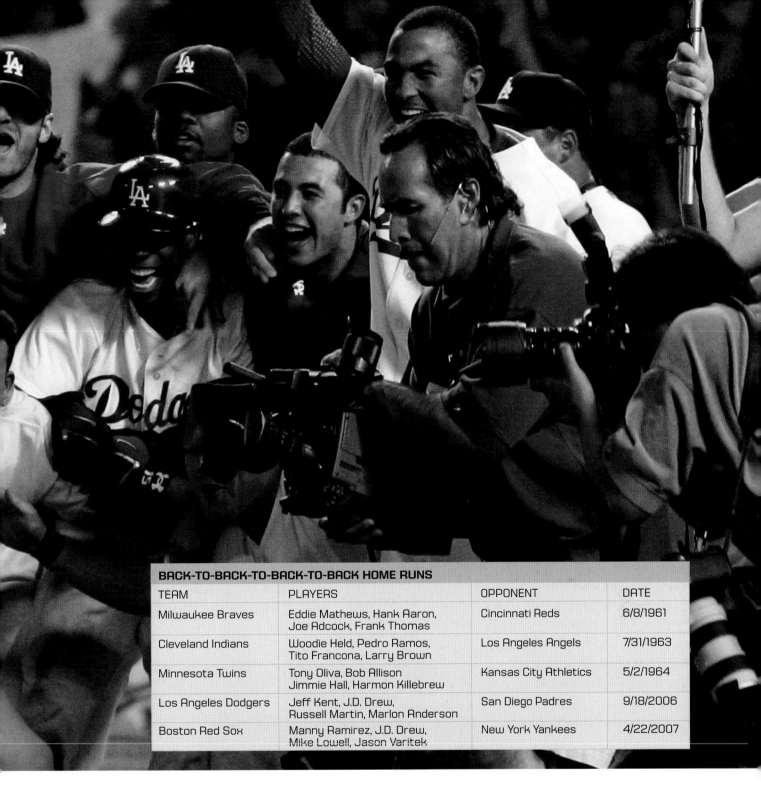

BACK-TO-BACK-TO-BACK-TO-BACK HOME RUNS			
TEAM	PLAYERS	OPPONENT	DATE
Milwaukee Braves	Eddie Mathews, Hank Aaron, Joe Adcock, Frank Thomas	Cincinnati Reds	6/8/1961
Cleveland Indians	Woodie Held, Pedro Ramos, Tito Francona, Larry Brown	Los Angeles Angels	7/31/1963
Minnesota Twins	Tony Oliva, Bob Allison Jimmie Hall, Harmon Killebrew	Kansas City Athletics	5/2/1964
Los Angeles Dodgers	Jeff Kent, J.D. Drew, Russell Martin, Marlon Anderson	San Diego Padres	9/18/2006
Boston Red Sox	Manny Ramirez, J.D. Drew, Mike Lowell, Jason Varitek	New York Yankees	4/22/2007

figured it was too little, too late. J.D. Drew followed with another, forcing the Padres to bring in Trevor Hoffman, who was 55 for 57 against L.A in save chances. Rookie Russell Martin greeted him by sending the first pitch out of the park for the third-straight homer.

Down by just one, L.A.'s Marlon Anderson got up and socked one, too. It was the fourth time a team had hit four consecutive shots, but the first time in the ninth, or to tie a game. "If the ghosts of Zach Wheat and Babe Herman rode through the gate in center field saddled high on the back of the Loch Ness Monster, it might not have been as shocking," the *Los Angeles Times*' Brian Kamenetzky wrote.

But they weren't done. After San Diego went ahead in the 10th, 10-9, Nomar Garciaparra answered with a walk-off, two-run homer, shooting the Dodgers from half a game behind the Padres to half a game ahead. Los Angeles would go on to win the Wild Card.

Clarke

CORSICANA OIL CITYS VS. TEXARKANA CASKETMAKERS
JUNE 15, 1902

THE TOWN OF CORSICANA, TEXAS, was just a dusty spot in the middle of nowhere until 1894, when it became the site of the state's first major oil strike. Money and people poured in, and soon its population could support a team in the Class D Texas League, the lowest level of the Minors. Well-financed, the club attracted the talent that the rest of the ramshackle Texas League couldn't. The Oil Citys posted an 87-23 record in 1902, winning the pennant by nearly 30 games. At one point they won 27 straight, a record that would stand for 85 years.

But, never was Corsicana more dominant than on June 15, 1902, in a matchup against the Texarkana Casketmakers at a tiny Ennis ballpark. Corsicana's blue laws outlawed Sunday baseball, forcing the team to play its Sunday games in the nearby town of Ennis, where the outfield fences sat as close as 140 feet from home plate. Texarkana's club was in such bad shape that the owner's son had to pitch, leading to an unbelievable 51-3 Corsicana win. The Oil Citys collected 53 hits and knocked 21 homers over the comically shallow fences. The brightest star of the day was Justin "Nig" Clarke, a 19-year-old Canadian catcher, who collected eight home runs and 16 RBI. His phenomenal stat line got Big League attention. By 1905 Clarke was playing in Cleveland, but would end his nine-year Major League career with fewer lifetime home runs (six) than he hit on that Sunday afternoon in Ennis.

Ring

CUBS VS. PHILLIES
AUGUST 25, 1922

PITCHING COACHES VERY OFTEN emphasize that a pitcher must be mentally tough enough to block out distractions — including calls by the umpire. As Exhibit A they can cite Jimmy Ring, the Philadelphia pitcher whose frustration with the men in blue on Aug. 25, 1922, made possible the highest-scoring game in Major League history. Ring had a 3-1 lead on the Cubs in the second when he became frustrated with home plate ump Bob Hart. Unraveled, Ring gave up 10 runs in the frame, but Manager Kaiser Wilhelm left him on the mound to take the beating, figuring the game was out of reach anyway. Surprisingly, Ring pitched a scoreless third, but he had to be pulled in the fourth when the Cubs' bats exploded again. By the end of that inning Chicago was ahead, 25-6.

Remarkably, the Phillies mounted one of the greatest comebacks ever, while their relievers held the Cubs to just one run over the last five innings. Chicago had begun to use the game as a sort of tryout, running out five rookie pitchers in a row, all of whom were raked over the coals by Phillie batters. The Phils scored eight in the eighth and six in the ninth, cutting the deficit to 26-23. They loaded the bases and brought the go-ahead run to the plate with two outs in the ninth, but Chicago rookie Tiny Osborne came through in the clutch and struck out center fielder Bevo LeBourveau to end it. Overall, the teams combined for 49 runs (a record), 51 hits, 21 walks and nine errors.

chapter 9
ALL-STAR GAMES

Despite the criticism that all-star exhibitions lack quality competition, it's clear that baseball, the inventor of the concept, is the best practitioner. Whether it's Super Bowl winners sitting out football's Pro Bowl or NBA stars who think defense is best saved for the playoffs, such games are often less than scintillating. Baseball, though, has staged some Midsummer Classics that are truly worthy of the title "classic," featuring walk-off home runs, virtuoso pitching performances and (as seen in the 1970 contest when Pete Rose validated his nickname as "Charlie Hustle") game-ending collisions at home plate.

TED WILLIAMS BRIGGS STADIUM 1941

AS WORLD WAR II LOOMED OVER THE NATION IN 1941, BASEBALL HAD an exciting season. Ted Williams chased .400, Joe DiMaggio hit in 56 straight games, and the Dodgers and Yankees faced off in the first Subway Series. But the most remarkable part of that summer may have been the All-Star Game in Detroit. The AL took a 2-1 lead in the sixth, but the NL roared back, claiming a 5-2 lead by the eighth on a pair of two-run shots by Pirates shortstop Arky Vaughan.

But the Junior Circuit did not go quietly. With one out in the bottom of the ninth, the AL loaded the bases on two singles and a walk, bringing up Joe DiMaggio as the winning run. He grounded to short for what could have been a game-ending double play, but he hustled down the line, beating the relay. That brought up Boston's Ted Williams as the AL's last chance against Cubs righty Claude Passeau. With the score at 5-4, "Ted had a great swing at a pitch and fouled it straight back," teammate Dom DiMaggio, Joe's brother, recalled. "It's funny, but I thought to myself, if he had hit that fair, it would have gone over the roof. Then he hit the ball off the roof." The 22-year-old Williams celebrated his way around the bases after hitting the first walk-off home run in All-Star Game history. "It wasn't a fly ball; it was a line drive that just went straight up and hit the roof on a line," DiMaggio said. "In all my years playing in that park, I never saw another one hit like that."

REGGIE JACKSON TIGER STADIUM 1971

ALTHOUGH SIX FUTURE HALL OF FAMERS HIT home runs in the 1971 All-Star Game, it's Reggie Jackson's titanic blast off the roof that years later still elicits chills. Overshadowing home runs by Frank Robinson, Harmon Killebrew, Hank Aaron, Roberto Clemente and Johnny Bench, Jackson's shot is still thought of as one of baseball's most memorable roundtrippers. "It has to be very close to the hardest hit ball I've ever seen," said Al Kaline, Jackson's American League teammate. "The ring off the bat was devastating. It was a noise you don't hear often — almost like an aluminum bat. There was a sound when he hit it, even in a noisy ballpark, that was unbelievable."

The future Mr. October was 25 years old in 1971 and playing in just his second All-Star Game. In the third inning, he came up against Pittsburgh's Dock Ellis and launched a ball so far that it appeared to still be going up when it crashed into a transformer that sat atop Tiger Stadium's roof. "I just wanted to get a base hit and prolong the rally," Jackson told the *Detroit News*. "Then Dock hung a mattress ball — a slider — and it was like hitting a golf shot on the sweet spot, like maybe the best shot of my life." Jackson's homer tied the game at 3-3 and propelled the AL to an eventual 6-4 victory. A local physics professor later estimated that the ball would have flown 510 feet had it not struck the transformer.

JOHNNY CALLISON SHEA STADIUM 1964

IN 1964, THE NATIONAL LEAGUE WAS SMACK IN THE middle of one of the most dominant runs either league has ever enjoyed in the All-Star Game — a period in which it would go 13 games and 11 years without a loss. (Two games each were played during 1960 and '61.) So even when the Senior Circuit entered the ninth inning of the 1964 contest trailing, 4-3, most people figured it would find a way to pull it out. It came as no surprise, then, when Willie Mays, as *The New York Times* put it, "scored the tying run almost single-handedly — or, more accurately, single-footedly."

Facing Dick Radatz, Boston's relief ace, Mays fouled off six pitches before leading off the ninth with a walk. He then stole

second, advanced to third on Orlando Cepeda's bloop single and scored as a precautionary throw home skipped past the cutoff man. With one out, AL Manager Al Lopez took a risk: intentionally walking Johnny Edwards to get to Hank Aaron, hoping Aaron would hit into a double play. The Hammer struck out instead, bringing up Philadelphia's Johnny Callison. The 25-year-old slugger ripped a drive down the right-field line. Plenty far enough to be a homer, the only question was whether it would be fair or foul. It stayed fair, and just like that the All-Star Game was over. The win enabled the Senior Circuit to tie the all-time series record; it would take the lead the next year and hold it for decades.

HANK BLALOCK U.S. CELLULAR FIELD 2003

GETTING A HIT IN THE ALL-STAR GAME IS TOUGH ENOUGH WHEN you're facing top-flight pitchers you see just once a year, if you're lucky. But 22-year-old Hank Blalock's task in 2003 was even more daunting: get a pinch-hit off a pitcher he had never faced before *and* who was enjoying the most dominant relief pitching season in the history of baseball. Eric Gagne had saved 38 straight games entering the All-Star Game, but that was just the tip of the iceberg. By the time his streak was over, he would save an incredible 84 in a row. His ERA for the 2003 season would end up at 1.20, the lowest in history for a closer throwing at least 80 innings. Gagne also would set two new Major League records by averaging just 4.04 hits and 14.98 strikeouts per nine innings.

The first sign that something was awry for the NL came in the bottom of the eighth, when Manager Dusty Baker decided to use baseball's best closer as a set-up man out of deference to veteran closer John Smoltz. Perhaps struggling in the unfamiliar role, Gagne quickly gave up two doubles. Blalock stepped into the batter's box as a pinch-hitter with the AL trailing, 6-5, and the tying run on second. Remarkably, he pounded one of Gagne's famous fastballs into the seats, giving the AL its winning margin and becoming just the 12th player to homer in his first career All-Star Game at-bat. "In a situation like that you can barely feel yourself run around the bases. I was just trying to get around without tripping," Blalock said. "That was my first time seeing Gagne, besides seeing him on *SportsCenter*."

ALL-STAR GAME CAREER RECORDS

STAT	PLAYER	TOTAL
Home Runs	Stan Musial	6
Hits	Willie Mays	23
RBI	Ted Williams	12
Starts	Don Drysdale/ Lefty Gomez/Robin Roberts	5
Wins	Lefty Gomez	3
Strikeouts	Don Drysdale	19

Holliday (sliding),
Barrett

chapter 10

CLINCHING GAMES

Every baseball season is filled with impressive performances, but it's often the specific player who comes through during an exciting pennant race that becomes a legend: Addie Joss, who pitched a perfect game near the end of the fabulous 1908 race, or Orel Hershiser, who didn't allow a run in September 1988 as his Dodgers fought to clinch the division crown. Perhaps the most impressive of all was Houston's Mike Scott, who pitched a no-hitter to clinch the NL West title for the Astros in 1986 — likely deciding the Cy Young Award in the process.

COLORADO ROCKIES   OCTOBER 1, 2007

BY THE SUMMER OF 2007, THE ROCKIES HAD GOTTEN USED TO BEING also-rans, finishing last or next-to-last in the NL West for 11 straight years. So it seemed just another ho-hum season in Colorado when, on Sept. 18, they were in fourth place again. That night, however, the Rockies started a streak of inspired baseball, beginning with a four-game sweep of the Dodgers, followed by a sweep of the Padres and another sweep of the Dodgers. The Rockies began their last series of the regular season on Sept. 28, just one game behind Wild Card leading San Diego. Facing the NL West leading Diamondbacks, Colorado won two of three, which was good enough to force a one-game playoff against the Padres.

The game was tense, tied, 6-6, after nine. San Diego put runners in scoring position in the 10th, 11th and 12th to no avail, but broke through in the 13th, taking an 8-6 lead on a Scott Hairston homer. In response, the Rockies mounted a comeback in the bottom of the 13th. Batting against all-time-saves leader Trevor Hoffman, Kaz Matsui and Troy Tulowitzki hit back-to-back doubles, followed by a Matt Holliday triple, to make it 8-8. After an intentional walk to Todd Helton, Jamey Carroll lined out to right. Holliday tagged and crashed home headfirst into catcher Michael Barrett's shin guard. Called safe, a woozy, bleeding Holliday was mobbed by teammates as the Padres argued he never touched home. The Rockies won the Wild Card, and would ride their hot streak to the Fall Classic. "September has been like sending your kids out in the backyard to watch them play," Manager Clint Hurdle told the *Rocky Mountain News*. "You get real proud of the way they battled."

ONE-GAME PLAYOFFS	
TEAMS	DATE
Indians 8, Red Sox 3	10/4/1948
Yankees 5, Red Sox 4	10/2/1978
Astros 7, Dodgers 1	10/6/1980
Mariners 9, Angels 1	10/2/1995
Cubs 5, Giants 3	9/28/1998
Mets 5, Reds 0	10/4/1999
Rockies 9, Padres 8	10/1/2007

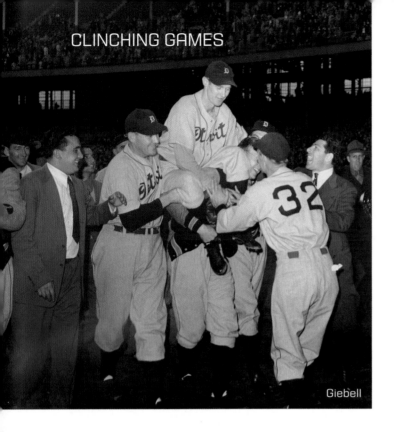

Giebell

DETROIT TIGERS
SEPTEMBER 27, 1940

ALTHOUGH CLEVELAND'S BOB FELLER BEGAN THE 1940 season in spectacular fashion, pitching an Opening Day no-hitter, his last start that year was memorable for a different reason. The Indians, trying to hold on to first place down the stretch, were overtaken by Detroit on Sept. 20. With two games left, Feller faced the Tigers in a must-win game on Sept. 27. "Rapid Robert" threw a spectacular three-hit, complete game — only to lose, 2-0, to Floyd Giebell, a 30-year-old career Minor Leaguer making his second Big League start.

It was a surprise that Giebell, called up from Buffalo a week earlier, even got the chance to start. "This morning, I called a meeting of my older players and asked them for their opinion on the day's pitching selection," Tigers Manager Del Baker said. "Their unanimous choice was Giebell." Early in the game it seemed Detroit might win by forfeit because Cleveland's Ladies' Day crowd showed its dislike for the rival Tigers by pelting star Hank Greenberg and his teammates with food and garbage. Detroit's bullpen catcher, Birdie Tebbetts, even required medical attention after getting knocked down by a basket of tomatoes.

After things settled down, the Tigers' Rudy York crushed a two-run homer for the only runs of the day. It was all Giebell needed, scattering just six hits and striking out six in clinching the pennant. Ineligible for the World Series because of his late recall, Giebell only got two more starts in his Big League career.

SILVER BATTING
TITLE AWARD

BOSTON RED SOX   OCTOBER 1, 1967

IN 1967, TWO YEARS BEFORE THE START OF DIVISIONAL play, the AL enjoyed its last wide-open pennant race. Going into the season's final weekend, Chicago, Detroit, Minnesota and the "Impossible Dream" Red Sox were all in the hunt. Moreover, Boston's Carl Yastrzemski was on one of the great hot streaks of all time and in pursuit of the Triple Crown. Yaz had comfortable leads in the batting and RBI races, but was battling for the home

run crown with the Twins' Harmon Killebrew. Tied at 43 on the second-to-last day of the season, each man homered once to remain tied at 44. The Triple Crown, like the pennant, would be decided on the last day of the season. Chicago had been eliminated the previous day, so when the Sox and Twins faced off at Fenway they only needed to watch for the scores of the Tigers-Angels double-header. Meanwhile, Yaz continued his hot hitting, going 4 for 4 with two RBI as Boston's Jim Lonborg pitched a complete-game to defeat the Twins, 5-3. Neither Yastrzemski nor Killebrew went deep, so their tie for the home run title enabled Yaz to claim the Triple Crown. Over the last two weeks of the pennant race, the Sox left fielder had batted a remarkable .523 with five homers and 16 RBI in 12 games, making him an easy choice for AL MVP. Boston claimed the pennant that day, but lost the World Series in seven.

DETROIT TIGERS
SEPTEMBER 30, 1945

WHEN HANK GREENBERG WAS drafted into the military in 1941, he was 30 years old, the reigning American League Most Valuable Player and was playing for the defending AL-champion Detroit Tigers. After four-and-a-half years overseas, Greenberg had missed more than 650 games, and reached the age when most players begin to decline. In response to questions about whether he would ever resemble the player he had been before his long layoff, Greenberg hit a home run in his first game back on July 1, 1945.

In late September, Greenberg's Tigers were neck-and-neck with Washington's Senators for the pennant, and could clinch the title by beating the St. Louis Browns on the season's last day. The game, played on a rain-soaked field at Sportsman's Park in St. Louis, absolutely lived up to all the hype. Down 3-2 in the ninth inning with two runners on, St. Louis intentionally walked mediocre hitter Doc Cramer to face Greenberg with the bases loaded. Greenberg made them pay. "Never was a title won in more dramatic fashion," wrote an AP reporter. "A light mist was falling as big Hank stepped up with his team a run behind and gave one of Nelson Potter's screwballs a tremendous ride into the bleachers." As Greenberg rounded the bases after hitting his AL pennant-winning blast, he recalled, his teammates "pounded me on the back, and carried on like I was a hero."

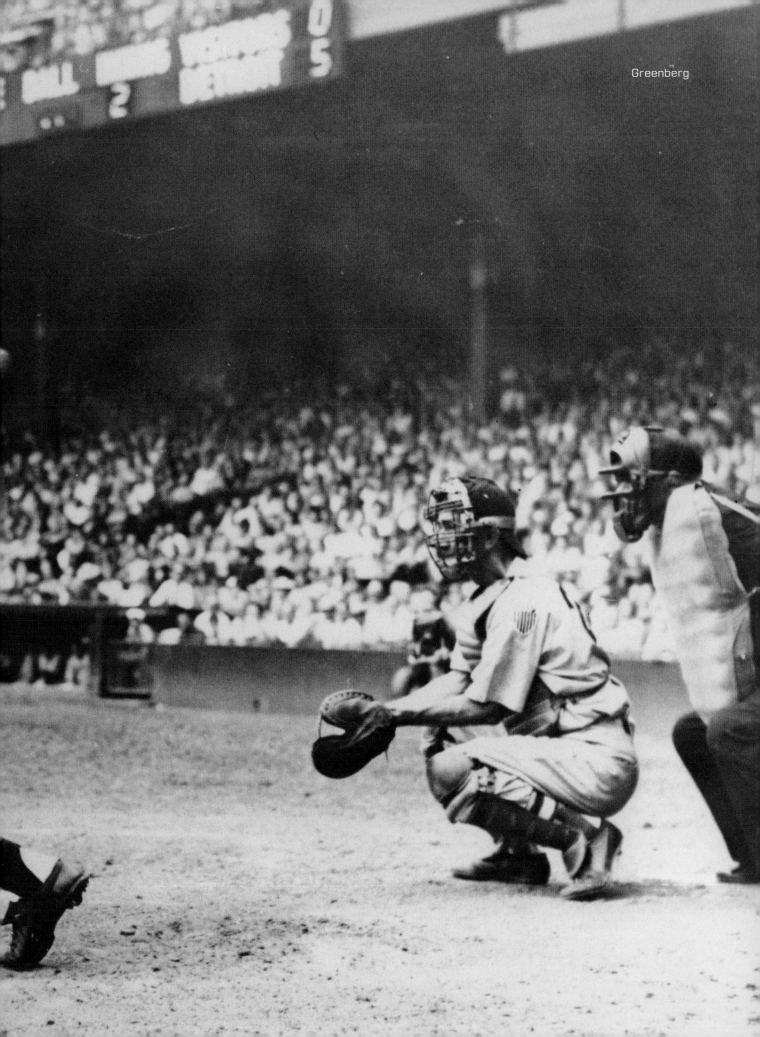

Greenberg

chapter 11

DIVISION SERIES

Although the Division Series is not as steeped in history and folklore as the Fall Classic or the League Championship Series, it already has provided a good deal of great games, silencing even those old-school critics who grumbled about its creation. Its signature moment thus far may have come in 1999, when the Indians and Red Sox played a winner-take-all Game 5 at Jacobs Field in Cleveland. Pedro Martinez, the best pitcher in baseball at the time, was scratched from the lineup due to a back injury, but entered the game in relief anyway. All he did was turn in one of the finest clutch pitching performances of all time, throwing six no-hit innings to help the Sox sew up the series. "We've got a lot of heart on this team," outfielder Troy O'Leary said. "Pedro showed it."

ASTROS VS. BRAVES 2005 NLDS, GAME 4

IN ORDER TO STAY ALIVE, THE ATLANTA Braves had no choice but to win Game 4 of the 2005 Division Series at Houston's Minute Maid Park. The Braves led, 6-1, late in the game, but Astros slugger Lance Berkman crushed an eighth-inning grand slam, narrowing the margin to 6-5. Then in the bottom of the ninth, light-hitting Houston catcher Brad Ausmus, of all people, homered to send the game into extra innings. From that point on, each team struggled to score in what seemed a never-ending contest. The Astros placed the winning run in scoring position in the 10th and 15th innings to no avail, while Atlanta did the same in the 10th, 11th, 12th, 14th and 17th. Most painful was the top of the 14th, when the Braves loaded the

bases with just one out against Astros right-handed reliever Dan Wheeler, only to have Brian McCann strike out and Pete Orr ground out.

Things turned bizarre in the 16th when Wheeler was relieved by 43-year-old Roger Clemens, who surrendered just one hit in three innings and came up to bat in the bottom of the 18th. Clemens struck out, but the next batter, Chris Burke, mercifully homered to end the game and the series. It was the longest contest in postseason history, and only the seventh time a player had ended a playoff series with a home run. (The others were Bill Mazeroski, Chris Chambliss, Joe Carter, Todd Pratt, Aaron Boone and David Ortiz.) "It was kind of a microcosm of our season," Burke said. "Started out slow, finished strong."

Posada (left), Giambi

YANKEES VS. ATHLETICS
2001 ALDS, GAME 3

ENTERING OCTOBER 2001, THE Yankees had won four of the last five world titles, and most of them pretty easily. But now they faced a tough test: Trailing Oakland, 2-games-to-none, in the Division Series, the Yanks were on the verge of being swept out of the playoffs for the first time since 1980. They needed to win three straight, starting with Game 3 in Oakland.

Fortunately for New York, its newly signed ace, Mike Mussina, was on his game. The Stanford alum threw seven masterful innings, scattering four hits and allowing just two men to reach scoring position. One was Jeremy Giambi, who singled with two outs in the seventh. On what would be Mussina's last pitch of the game, Terrence Long doubled to right. Giambi, a fine hitter but notoriously slow base runner, lumbered toward home plate. It looked as though he would score when Shane Spencer's off-line throw sailed past the cutoff man. But at the last moment, shortstop Derek Jeter swooped in, cut the ball off near the first base line and flipped it back toward home. A stunned Giambi, who almost certainly would have scored had he slid, was tagged out standing up by Jorge Posada. Jeter's play energized the Yankees, who would go on to win both the ALDS and ALCS before losing in the World Series to Arizona. "A shortstop making that play behind first base, in foul territory," Jeter's teammate Luis Sojo marveled, "you're not going to see that play ever again."

MARINERS VS. YANKEES 1995 ALDS, GAME 5

BY 1995, THE YANKEES HAD GONE 14 YEARS without making the postseason — their longest such stretch since acquiring Babe Ruth. Recent years had been marked by turmoil, but the 1995 team looked different. Center fielder Bernie Williams came into his own, and Minor League call-ups Derek Jeter, Mariano Rivera and Jorge Posada showed promise. New York captured the Wild Card and hoped to reach the World Series for the sake of aging team captain Don Mattingly, whose career started in 1982, thus spanning the playoff drought.

The Division Series came down to a winner-take-all Game 5 against the Mariners. New York took a 4-2 lead into the eighth, but David Cone imploded that inning, allowing Seattle to the game tie on a Ken Griffey Jr. home run and a bases-loaded walk. The Yanks threatened in the ninth, but Seattle responded by bringing in Randy Johnson in relief. Johnson mowed down the Yanks, getting six straight outs, including four strikeouts. But eventually he tired, allowing New York to score in the 11th. The Yankees' elation was short-lived, however, as Jack McDowell, in his first-ever relief effort, never recorded an out in the bottom of the inning. Joey Cora and Griffey singled, and Edgar Martinez doubled to the left-field corner. Griffey, speeding around the bases, slid home safely to score the series-winning run. Although the Yankees were crestfallen, they knew they'd just participated in a classic. "It was one hell of a series," Cone said, "for the fans and for baseball."

chapter 12

LEAGUE CHAMPIONSHIP SERIES

When baseball split into divisions in 1969, many feared the pennant race would become a thing of the past. Hardly. That first year of divisional play featured a barn-burner of a three-team race in the NL West, and the "Miracle Mets" came from 9.5 games behind to win the NL East. The League Championship Series has provided some of baseball's most thrilling moments. In 1997 alone, Livan Hernandez struck out a record 15 batters to top Greg Maddux in the NLCS, while the ALCS boasted a classic duel between Mike Mussina and Orel Hershiser that lasted 12 innings and ended on a steal of home. Ah, just another year in the life of the LCS.

CARDINALS VS. DODGERS   1985 NLCS, GAME 5

ALTHOUGH OZZIE SMITH WAS ONE OF baseball's best players, power was never his forte. Entering the 1985 playoffs, the switch-hitter had just 12 career home runs — every one of them off of a left-handed pitcher. So when Smith came up against right-handed reliever Tom Niedenfuer on Oct. 14, 1985, with Game 5 of the National League Championship Series on the line and the series tied at two games apiece, few were prepared for the shocking event that took place.

Niedenfuer retired Willie McGee to lead off the bottom of the ninth and then got two strikes on Smith. Unafraid of Smith's power, even in a tied game, Niedenfuer gave him an inside fastball, and the diminutive shortstop pulled it down the line and just over the fence for a walk-off homer. "Go

crazy, folks! Go crazy!" broadcaster Jack Buck told Cardinals fans — and they did. "It's the last thing you'd expect to win a game," Niedenfuer said. "If you'd ask him, he'd be as surprised as I am."

"I was pretty surprised," Smith admitted. "I wasn't trying to win the game today with a homer ... I was just trying to get an extra-base hit." Unfortunately for the Dodgers, it wasn't the last dramatic home run Niedenfuer would surrender in the '85 NLCS. Back in L.A. for Game 6, he gave up a three-run, ninth-inning shot to Jack Clark that wrapped up the NLCS for the Cardinals. But Smith's homer still remained the most shocking. "If someone's going to hit a home run against you," Niedenfuer said, "you think about Clark, [Cesar] Cedeno, [Tom] Herr. Certainly not Ozzie Smith."

Smith (left)

BRAVES VS. PIRATES 1992 NLCS, GAME 7

IN 1992, NOBODY EXPECTED FRANCISCO CABRERA to make Atlanta's playoff roster. Cabrera was the Braves' third- or fourth-string catcher, behind Greg Olson, Damon Berryhill and perhaps even rookie Javy Lopez. But when Olson broke his leg, Atlanta decided to play it safe and carry the other three catchers on its postseason roster.

Entering the bottom of the ninth in Game 7 of the NLCS, the Braves' season appeared over, as they trailed, 2-0, against former Cy Young winner Doug Drabek. But Atlanta rallied, and Drabek was relieved by Stan Belinda. A sacrifice fly cut Pittsburgh's lead to 2-1. With the bases loaded and two outs, Belinda needed to retire just one more batter — Cabrera, who was pinch-hitting for the

pitcher — to end the game and the series. The series ended, all right, but not as the Pirates had hoped. Instead, Cabrera roped a single to left. The tying run scored from third while the sluggish Sid Bream chugged around the bases, trying to score the game-winner from second. The throw from left fielder Barry Bonds was accurate but a hair late, and Bream slid home with the pennant-

winning run by the slimmest of margins. "I don't play every day," Cabrera said in an understatement. "When I get the opportunity, I am ready." Remarkably, Cabrera's feat of snatching victory from the jaws of defeat is unique in all of baseball history. No other player has ever come through with a series-ending hit when his team's season would have ended if he made an out.

Chambliss

YANKEES VS. ROYALS 1976 ALCS, GAME 5

ALTHOUGH IT MAY BE HARD TO BELIEVE TODAY, during the late 1970s one of the best rivalries in baseball was between the Yankees and the Royals. Although they played in separate divisions, the clubs faced each other in the American League Championship Series four times in five years. The most memorable matchup came in 1976, when the teams split the first four games of the best-of-five ALCS, leading to a winner-take-all contest at Yankee Stadium.

It looked like smooth sailing for the Yankees, as they held a 6-3 lead entering the eighth. But the first two Royals batters singled, bringing up AL batting champ George Brett as the tying run.

Brett blasted a homer into the right-field stands, tying the score, 6-6. "We weren't down," the Yankees' Chris Chambliss said. "It just tied the game. We knew we had to score some more runs."

Leading off the bottom of the ninth, Chambliss swung at the first pitch and sent it into the stands for a pennant-winning homer. Fans rushed the field as Chambliss circled the bases. He touched second with his hand, and ran a circuitous route from there, dodging obstacles and getting knocked down. "Home plate was completely covered with people," he said. "I wasn't sure if I tagged it or not. I came in the clubhouse and all the players were talking about whether I got it. I wasn't sure, so I went back out and tagged it."

Fernandez, circling the bases after homering off Benitez

INDIANS VS. ORIOLES
1997 ALCS, GAME 6

WHEN THE ORIOLES FELL BEHIND, 3-games-to-2, in the 1997 ALCS, they remained confident — their ace, Mike Mussina, would be pitching against the Indians in Game 6 at Camden Yards. Winner of 54 games over the prior three seasons, Mussina came through in style. He pitched eight innings of shutout ball, struck out 10 and allowed just one hit, a David Justice double. But Cleveland starter Charles Nagy, though not as overwhelming as Mussina, held the O's in check, keeping Baltimore scoreless despite allowing nine hits and striking out just four. At the end of nine innings, the game remained a scoreless tie.

With their season hanging in the balance, the Orioles sent volatile young set-up man Armando Benitez to the mound for the 11th inning. Benitez, just 24, had posted a 2.45 ERA and struck out an astounding 106 batters in 73.1 innings. But he had also developed a reputation for instability, which included giving up a disputed game-tying homer to Derek Jeter — or, rather, to Jeffrey Maier — in the previous year's ALCS. Benitez was tagged again, this time when veteran infielder Tony Fernandez crushed a hanging slider over the right-field scoreboard for what would be the only run of the game. The Orioles, with the AL's best record at 98-64, were sent packing. "This whole series I didn't think we caught many breaks," O's Manager Davey Johnson lamented. "We're champions in my eyes. I'm just sorry that we didn't get to the final dance."

Orosco

METS VS. ASTROS 1986 NLCS, GAME 6

ALTHOUGH THE ASTROS TRAILED THE METS, 3-games-to-2, in the 1986 NLCS, they weren't worried. Houston would play the final two games at home in the Astrodome, and if the Astros could just survive Game 6, they had soon-to-be Cy Young winner Mike Scott ready for Game 7. Scott had utterly dominated the Mets to that point, pitching complete-game victories in each of his two starts while posting a 0.50 ERA.

Until the ninth inning of Game 6 everything was going as planned for Houston. They led, 3-0, behind the dominant pitching of starter Bob Knepper. But Knepper crumbled in the ninth, and the Mets managed to tie. Extra innings started out quietly, as neither team placed a runner in scoring position until the 14th. In that inning,

New York took the lead on a Wally Backman single. The Astros, not to be outdone, retied it in the bottom of the frame on a Billy Hatcher home run, and the game continued. In the top of the 16th the Mets exploded, scoring three runs on hits by Ray Knight and Lenny Dykstra. Again, the Astros answered. With two outs, they put the tying run on second and the winning run on first. But closer Jesse Orosco, pitching a third successful inning, retired Houston's Kevin Bass to win the pennant. Orosco celebrated by throwing his glove high in the air. "I didn't want to have to beat Scott in the seventh game," the Mets' Keith Hernandez admitted. "Who knows what we would have done?" The Astros' ace was named NLCS MVP despite playing on the losing team.

Monday

DODGERS VS. EXPOS
1981 NLCS, GAME 5

OCTOBER 19, 1981, WAS A COLD and rainy day in Montreal, but that's not why it became known to Québécois as "Blue Monday." It was the day the Expos finally had the National League pennant in their grasp, only to have it snatched away. Montreal faced long odds in Game 5 of the NLCS against the Dodgers and soon-to-be Cy Young winner Fernando Valenzuela. The Expos scratched a run off him in the first, but Valenzuela buckled down, holding Montreal scoreless on two hits thereafter. The Dodgers tied it in the fifth, but the Expos still believed they would win if they could hold on until Valenzuela left the game. In the ninth, Montreal's ace, Steve Rogers, made his first relief appearance of the year. He retired sluggers Steve Garvey and Ron Cey, but then threw what *The New York Times* described as "a sinker that did not sink" to little-used Rick Monday. Monday homered, giving the Dodgers a 2-1 lead.

Valenzuela tried to complete his masterpiece but appeared fatigued in the ninth. When Fernando walked Gary Carter on his 113th pitch of the game, Dodgers Manager Tommy Lasorda brought in Bob Welch, usually a starter, to record the pennant-clinching out. "That was a young team with a lot of good players," Tim Raines later said of the 1981 Expos. "I thought we would be fighting for the pennant for the next 10 years." Although the Expos lasted 23 more seasons in Montreal, they would never come as close to a World Series as they had on "Blue Monday."

Bench

Maddox

REDS VS. PIRATES
1972 NLCS, GAME 5

FEW TEAMS KNOW LEAGUE CHAMPIONSHIP SERIES pain better than the Pittsburgh Pirates, who have lost in the LCS seven times since divisional play began in 1969. Although three straight losses from 1990–92 overshadow it, the dramatic 1972 series was likely the most painful. That season, Roberto Clemente's last, the Bucs came within three outs of the pennant only to let it slip away. Pittsburgh took a 3-2 lead into the ninth inning of the deciding Game 5, until reliever Dave Giusti gave up a tying homer to the first batter he faced, Johnny Bench. Both Tony Perez and Denis Menke followed with singles, and Bob Moose, trying to put out the fire, tantalized Pirates fans by recording two outs. But then he uncorked a wild pitch, allowing the winning run to score.

PHILLIES VS. ASTROS
1980 NLCS, GAME 5

AS THE DECISIVE GAME 5 OF THE 1980 NATIONAL League Championship Series neared its end, the Astros were on the brink of winning their first pennant. They broke a 2-2 tie with three runs off the Phillies in the seventh, and their big free-agent acquisition, Nolan Ryan, was cruising on the mound. But Ryan fell apart in the top of the eighth, giving up three hits and a walk before getting pulled. Following reliever Joe Sambito, Ken Forsch entered the inning and struck out Mike Schmidt, but then allowed the Phillies to go ahead. The Astros retied it in the eighth, but in the 10th, Philadelphia's Garry Maddox doubled just past the glove of diving center fielder Terry Puhl. "No question this is the biggest thrill I've ever had in baseball," Maddox said.

Gibson

chapter 13
WORLD SERIES

In 1901, the American League tried to establish itself as a bona fide equal to the National League. After years of resulting hostility between the two leagues, it became obvious that they could make fans happier — and earn more money — by settling their differences and organizing a postseason championship series. Thus the World Series was born. Since then (except in 1904 and 1994), it has been played on freezing nights and sunny afternoons, in cavernous domes and rickety wooden ballparks, by millionaires and by guys making $5,000 a year. But wherever and however it happens, the World Series will always be one of America's premier sporting events.

DODGERS VS. ATHLETICS
1988 WORLD SERIES, GAME 1

THE LOS ANGELES DODGERS, WHO ENTERED THE 1988 WORLD SERIES as underdogs against the juggernaut Oakland Athletics, became even more of a long shot when injuries benched soon-to-be NL MVP Kirk Gibson. Gibson had hurt both his right knee and left hamstring during the NLCS. It was no surprise, then, when Oakland took early control of Game 1 on a Jose Canseco grand slam and handed a 4-3 lead to Hall of Fame closer Dennis Eckersley. The first two Dodgers made outs in the ninth before pinch-hitter Mike Davis, a .196 batter, worked an unlikely walk (just Eck's 11th free pass that season). That brought up the pitcher's spot. Utility infielder Dave Anderson was sent to the on-deck circle as a decoy, but Dodgers Manager Tommy Lasorda had an idea.

The injured Gibson had been taking practice swings off a tee in the clubhouse, and to everyone's surprise, he limped to the plate with everything on the line. "We were going to win the game, and I was going to win it for us," he said later. "That's what I visualized." Gibson fought off pitch after pitch, but a weak hobble toward first base after a couple of foul grounders brought into question whether he could reach safely even on an outfield hit. As it turned out, he didn't need to. Eckersley, who, until then, had thrown only fastballs, tried to sneak in a 3-2 backdoor slider for strike three. But Gibby was ready, and with a one-handed swing, pulled it into the right-field pavilion for a walk-off — or, rather, limp-off — homer. It was not only the most dramatic and unlikely hit in World Series history, but also the Series' first come-from-behind, walk-off homer. To this day, Gibson remains the only man to hit a game-winning World Series home run in a situation in which his team would have lost if he made an out.

Clarkson

BROWNS VS. WHITE STOCKINGS 1886 WORLD SERIES, GAME 6

THE EARLY WORLD SERIES OF 1884–90 were played by the National League and American Association. Although it was considered inferior, the AA proved itself in the 1886 championship, when the St. Louis Browns defeated the Chicago White Stockings. Game 6 featured a duel between legendary hurlers John Clarkson and Bob Caruthers. Clarkson's Stockings led, 3-0, until St. Louis tied it with an eighth-inning rally. In the bottom of the 10th, the Browns' Curt Welch singled, advanced on a hit and a steal, and then danced off third as if about to take home. Perhaps distracted, Clarkson threw a wild pitch and Welch scored the world series-winning run. His dash became known as the "$15,000 Slide" — named for the gate receipts the Browns players won.

Ruth (sliding), Hornsby

CARDINALS VS. YANKEES 1926 WORLD SERIES, GAME 7

WHEN NEW YORK LOADED THE bases at Yankee Stadium with two outs late in Game 7 of the 1926 World Series, St. Louis put in aged ace Grover Cleveland "Pete" Alexander to quell the threat. Even after a complete-game victory the day before, he struck out slugger Tony Lazzeri and preserved the 3-2 lead. But the Yanks weren't done. In the ninth, Babe Ruth walked, the first base runner allowed by Alexander, and Bob Meusel came up. The Babe, hoping to catch St. Louis by surprise, tried to put the tying run in scoring position by taking second base. The Cardinals weren't fooled, though, and they easily threw him out. It's the only time that the World Series has ended with a player caught stealing.

BLUE JAYS VS. PHILLIES 1993 WORLD SERIES, GAME 6

MITCH WILLIAMS WAS ONE OF THE BEST CLOSERS IN the NL in 1993, recording 43 saves with a respectable 3.34 ERA. But his 44 walks, as well as a propensity for control issues, earned him the nickname "Wild Thing," and fans of the NL-champion Phillies crossed their fingers when he entered a game. By the time Philadelphia reached Game 6 of the World Series against Toronto, Williams had blown three of six postseason save opportunities and retired the side in order just once. "He doesn't have ulcers," Manager Jim Fregosi quipped, "but he's one of the biggest carriers there is."

Now with the Phillies trailing, 3-games-to-2, but up, 6-5, in the bottom of the ninth, Williams entered the most important contest of his career. Phillies fans cringed as he walked base-stealer extraordinaire Rickey Henderson to lead off the inning. But before Henderson even got a chance to go, Paul Molitor had singled him over. That brought up Joe Carter, whose reputation as a clutch hitter made him the last man Williams wanted to face. The slugger worked the count to 2-2 before Williams threw a hanging slider that Carter knocked over the SkyDome's left-field fence. Carter half-ran, half-jumped around the bases, having hit just the second World Series-ending homer in history. "You always hope it's you in that situation," Carter said. "These are the kind of moments you dream about. ... They haven't made up the word yet to describe what the feeling is."

ATHLETICS VS. CUBS 1929 WORLD SERIES, GAME 4

THINGS LOOKED HOPELESS FOR THE PHILADELPHIA A's in Game 4 of the 1929 World Series as they fell behind, 8-0, to the Cubs. Further damage was avoided in the seventh, though, thanks to infielders Jimmy Dykes and Max Bishop, who turned an acrobatic double play that *The New York Times* called "a marvel of fielding, speed and precision." The play set the stage for the bottom of the frame, when the A's pulled off the biggest comeback in Series history — a deluge that "swept the Cubs before it like driftwood," as the *Times'* William Brandt aptly put it.

The A's Al Simmons led off with a towering homer that sailed over the left-field roof. His teammates followed with five singles,

knocking pitcher Charley Root out of the game. Then came a freak occurrence aided by the layout of the A's ballpark. Throughout the summer the sun sets in the northwest, but in autumn it sets more toward the southwest; at Shibe Park that meant October was the only time of year the sun shone directly into the center fielder's eyes. The Athletics' Mule Haas lifted a high fly ball directly at center fielder Hack Wilson, who, though no defensive wizard, ordinarily would have caught it. Instead he was blinded as the ball whizzed past him. Haas's inside-the-park homer opened the floodgates. By the inning's end, the A's had scored 10 runs and taken a 10-8 lead. The win put them up, 3-games-to-1, in the Series, which they won two days later.

COUNSELL'S
SPIKES

MARLINS VS. INDIANS
1997 WORLD SERIES, GAME 7

EVEN THOUGH CRITICS OF THE Marlins' 1997 championship claim Florida "bought" the World Series, that's only half the story. The team did feature expensive free agents like Kevin Brown, Moises Alou and Bobby Bonilla, but the Fish wouldn't have gone far without three youngsters: Charles Johnson, Edgar Renteria and Livan Hernandez. That dynamic brought the Marlins to Game 7 of the World Series, where they found themselves down, 2-1, to Cleveland in the bottom of the ninth.

The Marlins staged a rally against closer Jose Mesa to tie the score, 2-2. In the 11th, Bonilla singled and advanced to third when Tony Fernandez booted a Craig Counsell ground ball. But after an intentional walk, Bonilla was forced out at home. That would have been the last out of the game, but thanks to the error, Renteria got up with two outs and the bases juiced. The 22-year-old shortstop singled to center field, driving in Counsell to end the Series. Once again, the youngsters came through, this time helping the Marlins become the first Wild Card team to win the World Series. Renteria and Johnson combined to hit .322 with six RBI during the series, while Hernandez won two games and was named MVP.

125

Slaughter

CARDINALS VS. RED SOX 1946 WORLD SERIES, GAME 7

ENOS SLAUGHTER HAD ENOUGH ATHLETICISM TO make him a Hall of Famer, but it was his fearless style of play that made him famous. This was never more evident than in 1946, when Slaughter's speed brought the Cardinals to a sixth world championship and sent the Boston Red Sox to a crushing defeat. Thanks to two incredible catches by center fielder Terry Moore, St. Louis held a 3-1 lead in the seventh inning of Game 7. The Red Sox caught up in the eighth on a game-tying double by Dom DiMaggio, but he twisted his ankle rounding first and had to leave the game.

Slaughter led off the eighth with a single and was still standing on first two outs later when Harry Walker slapped a hit to the gap in left-center. Had he still been in the game, DiMaggio, a spectacular

defensive center fielder, likely would have prevented Slaughter from scoring. Instead the ball was fielded by his replacement, Leon Culberson, and Slaughter kept on running. He slid home, scoring the go-ahead run, barely beating shortstop Johnny Pesky's relay throw to the plate. The Cardinals wrapped up the Series the next inning, and the deciding play became known as "Slaughter's Mad Dash." Red Sox fans were quick to blame the loss on Pesky, who was reported to have hesitated in between catching the throw from the outfield and relaying it home. But film of the play has revealed this claim to be unfounded. The Cardinals, of course, didn't care either way. "I just had to run, that was all," Slaughter said. "I just dug in and tore for home. … It was the Sox's responsibility to head me off."

Baker

Snodgrass

ATHLETICS VS. GIANTS
1911 WORLD SERIES, GAME 3

GAME 3 OF THE 1911 WORLD SERIES, WROTE *Sporting Life*'s Francis Richter, "has had no equal in World Series history." Through eight, Giants ace Christy Mathewson led the A's Jack Coombs, 1-0, but in the ninth Mathewson gave up a game-tying shot to Frank Baker, a prodigy who led the league with 11 longballs. In the 10th, the Giants' Fred Snodgrass flew into Baker at third with spikes high in retaliation. After being booed by his own fans, Snodgrass watched the A's bring the score to 3-1. In the bottom of the frame, Giants catcher Chief Meyers' near homer was blown foul by wind before Coombs retired the side. The A's won the Series and Baker earned the nickname "Home Run" Baker.

RED SOX VS. GIANTS
1912 WORLD SERIES, GAME 8

APPROPRIATELY FOR ONE OF THE MOST HOTLY contested Fall Classics ever, the 1912 World Series entered the 10th inning of the decisive game with the score tied, 1-1. In the top of the inning, Fred Merkle, famed goat of the Giants' 1908 season, smacked a go-ahead RBI hit. But Boston's Clyde Engle led off the bottom of the frame with an easy fly ball that was dropped by center fielder Fred Snodgrass. Snodgrass tried to atone by robbing the next batter of a potential triple, but the damage was done. The Giants infield flubbed a foul pop-up by Tris Speaker, who then singled to keep the game alive. Larry Gardner then drove in Boston's Series-winning run with a sacrifice fly, ensuring Snodgrass's infamy.

Buckner

METS VS. RED SOX 1986 WORLD SERIES, GAME 6

AFTER 68 YEARS, BOSTON'S FAMOUS TITLE DROUGHT appeared certain to end. Needing just one win to clinch, the Sox had a 3-2 lead in the eighth inning of Game 6 and baseball's best pitcher, Roger Clemens, on the mound. But Manager John McNamara took Clemens out — still a controversial move — and replaced him with Calvin Schiraldi, who promptly allowed the tying run. In the top of the 10th, however, Boston retook the lead on a Dave Henderson homer. In the bottom of the 10th inning, with Boston up, 5-3, McNamara played things a little differently. While he normally would have removed gimpy first baseman Bill Buckner, McNamara decided to leave Buckner in so he could be on the field for the final out.

Schiraldi retired the first two, but with just one more out to go for the championship, he allowed consecutive singles to Gary Carter, Kevin Mitchell and Ray Knight. Bob Stanley relieved and quickly made things worse with a wild pitch that scored the tying run and put the winning run on second. When the Mets' Mookie Wilson grounded down the first-base line, it still looked like Boston would get out alive. But Buckner let the ball bounce through his legs as the winning run scored. After such a crushing defeat, few were surprised when Boston lost, 8-5, in Game 7. "So close, yet so far," Stanley said. "This was my dream, to be out there when my team wins the world championship. I had a chance. Maybe I'll get another one."

Fisk

RED SOX VS. REDS 1975 WORLD SERIES, GAME 6

WHEN BOSTON ACE LUIS TIANT LEFT GAME 6 OF the '75 World Series trailing Cincinnati, 6-3, it looked like he would suffer his first-ever postseason loss. But Tiant was bailed out in the eighth by Sox pinch-hitter Bernie Carbo, who tied it up with a three-run shot. In the bottom of the ninth, Boston loaded the bases with no outs, but the Reds escaped with a double play. In the top of

the 11th with one out, Boston pulled off a doozy of its own. Dwight Evans made a terrific catch at the wall on a Joe Morgan fly and doubled up with a play at first.

Carlton Fisk led off the bottom of the 12th for the Sox at 12:33 a.m., and crushed a fly ball that bounced off the left-field foul pole for a game-winning homer. Even losing manager Sparky Anderson had to admit, "it was probably as good a ballgame as I've ever seen."

WORLD SERIES CAREER RECORDS		
STAT	PLAYER	TOTAL
Home Runs	Mickey Mantle	18
Hits	Yogi Berra	71
RBI	Mickey Mantle	40
Starts	Whitey Ford	22
Wins	Whitey Ford	10
Strikeouts	Whitey Ford	94

PIRATES VS. YANKEES
1960 WORLD SERIES,
GAME 7

SINCE THE 1960 WORLD SERIES was one of the highest-scoring Fall Classics ever, there were plenty of hitting heroes in both dugouts. The Yankees' Bobby Richardson set a record with 12 RBI. Mickey Mantle wasn't far behind, driving in 11 with a .400 average and three homers. But the two biggest hits came from unlikely Pirates: light-hitting second baseman Bill Mazeroski and backup catcher Hal Smith.

The Yanks outscored the Pirates, 46-17, in the first six games, but Pittsburgh managed a split, forcing a Game 7 at Forbes Field. It was a see-saw affair, with the Pirates taking an early 4-0 lead, only to lose it in the sixth. Down, 7-4, entering the bottom of the eighth, the Pirates rallied, aided by a bad hop that hit Yankees shortstop Tony Kubek in the throat, turning a potential double-play ball into a hit. With two outs, the Bucs took a two-run lead on a dramatic three-run homer by Smith. But the Yanks tied it right back up in the top of the ninth, on RBI hits by Mantle and Yogi Berra. The Pirates' leadoff man in the bottom half was Mazeroski, who had just 48 homers in his five-year career. Maz crushed a long fly ball, and Yankees left fielder Berra could only watch it fly over his head for the Series-ending home run. With one swing, the Pirates were champions. As Mazeroski circled the bases, a jubilant crowd celebrated the first Pirates championship in 35 years. "Everybody said we were dead," shortstop Dick Groat crowed. "We had a lot of chances to die, but didn't."

Mazeroski
(center)

Johnson

SENATORS VS. GIANTS
1924 WORLD SERIES,
GAME 7

AFTER SPENDING HIS ENTIRE career pitching for a team that was usually out of the race by midseason, the legendary Walter Johnson finally made it to the World Series in 1924 when his Senators brought home the first pennant in franchise history. With 377 career victories and a 23-7 record that season, Johnson was still the Senators' top pitcher at 36 years old. But the legend started the Series with a 12-inning, complete-game loss and got clobbered by the Giants in Game 5, losing 6-2. "Walter Johnson's great moment came," reporter Fred Lieb wrote after the latter game, "and it will leave a lifetime of tragic recollections."

Johnson, however, had another great moment up his sleeve. The Senators tied Game 7 in the eighth, 3-3, and the Big Train entered in relief on just one day's rest. He pitched masterfully, striking out five in four shutout innings. In the bottom of the 12th, Giants catcher Hank Gowdy tripped over his mask while chasing Muddy Ruel's foul pop-up. Ruel, given a second chance, knocked a double. Johnson batted for himself and reached on an error, bringing up rookie center fielder Earl McNeely, who hit a seemingly innocent grounder. But for the second time that day, a grounder improbably struck a pebble in Griffith Stadium's infield and hopped over the head of third baseman Freddie Lindstrom. Ruel scored the Series-winning run, while Johnson stood on second base and cried tears of joy. After 18 years, he was finally a world champion.

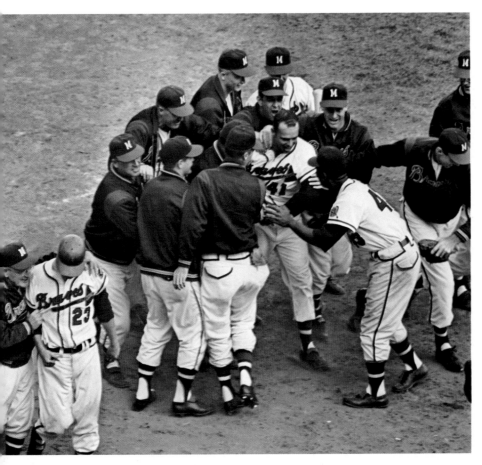

BRAVES VS. YANKEES
1957 WORLD SERIES, GAME 4

IN THE NINTH FRAME OF GAME 4 in the '57 World Series, Milwaukee ace Warren Spahn led, 4-1, and was one strike away from a complete-game masterpiece. But Elston Howard hit a three-run home run to send it into extra innings. Things got worse for Spahn in the 10th when the Yanks took the lead on a Hank Bauer RBI triple.

In the bottom of the frame, the Braves' Nippy Jones reached when a shoe polish stain on the ball proved he had been hit by a pitch. Johnny Logan then doubled, tying it up. Ordinarily, Yankees Manager Casey Stengel would have intentionally walked slugger Eddie Mathews, but he wanted to avoid facing Hank Aaron. Stengel's decision to pitch to Mathews backfired, resulting in a game-ending homer.

Terry

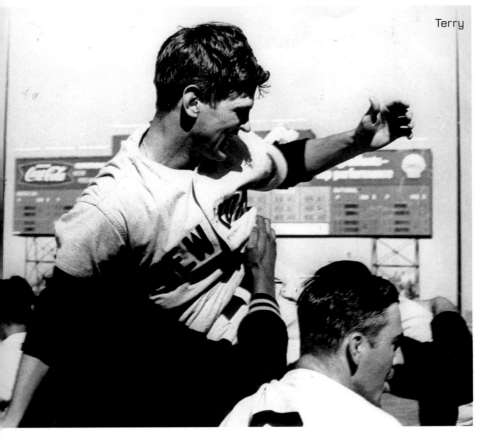

YANKEES VS. GIANTS
1962 WORLD SERIES, GAME 7

GAME 7 OF 1962's WORLD SERIES was a pitcher's dream, as Yankee Ralph Terry took a 1-0 lead into the bottom of the ninth at Candlestick Park. Matty Alou bunted for a single to lead off, but his brother Felipe and Chuck Hiller both struck out. That brought up Willie Mays as the Giants' last hope. Mays smacked a double, but the Yankees' Roger Maris made an excellent play in right field, forcing the Giants to hold the game-tying run at third. With first base open, Yankees Manager Ralph Houk made the decision for Terry to face dangerous lefty slugger Willie McCovey. "Stretch" hit a screaming line drive straight into the glove of second baseman Bobby Richardson, who staggered slightly but held on for the final out.

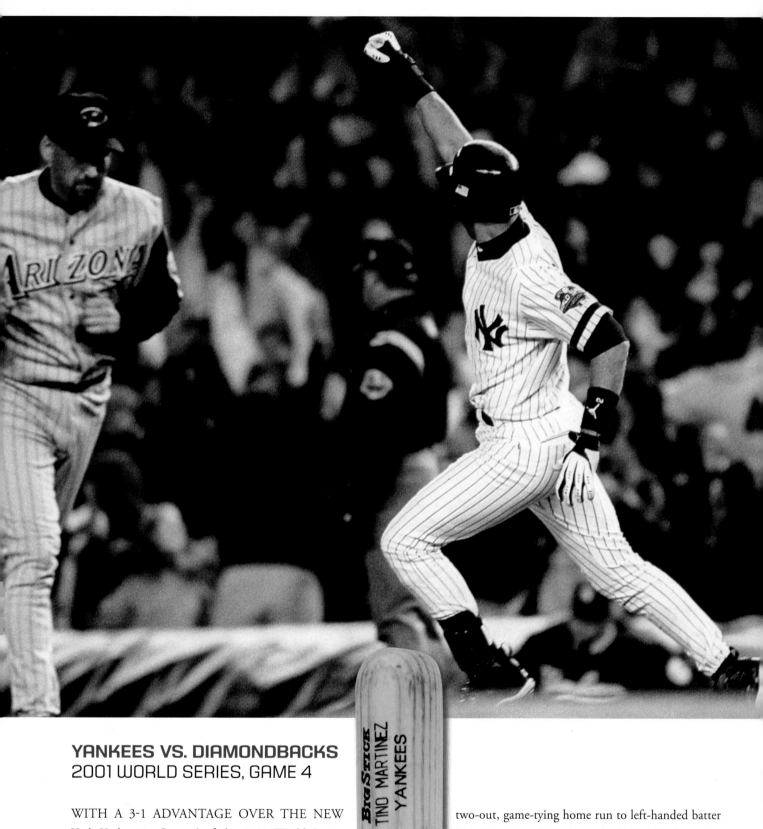

YANKEES VS. DIAMONDBACKS
2001 WORLD SERIES, GAME 4

WITH A 3-1 ADVANTAGE OVER THE NEW York Yankees in Game 4 of the 2001 World Series, Arizona Diamondbacks Manager Bob Brenly asked his outstanding closer, Byung-Hyun Kim, to pull off a two-inning save. Kim struck out the side in the eighth, but in the ninth inning gave up a dramatic, two-out, game-tying home run to left-handed batter Tino Martinez. "He threw the ball right down the middle to the wrong guy," said Kim's catcher, Damian Miller, after the game. "It's as simple as that." Yankee Stadium, Miller said, "was probably the loudest place I have heard as a player, after Tino hit that home run."

Jeter

DIAMONDBACKS VS. YANKEES
2001 WORLD SERIES, GAME 7

THE 2001 WORLD SERIES, ONE OF THE MOST exciting ever, appropriately ended in a thrilling Game 7 that featured as many as four future Hall of Fame pitchers. Veteran starters Roger Clemens and Curt Schilling each pitched well, as did Randy Johnson out of the Arizona bullpen. In the bottom of the ninth, the Yankees turned a 2-1 lead over to Mariano Rivera, who until then, easily had been the greatest pitcher in the history of postseason baseball. (In nearly 80 innings, he had posted a 6-0 record with 24 saves and a 0.70 ERA.) But after a single, a Rivera error and a double, Arizona had tied the game and put the winning run on third. New York was forced to play its infield in, making Luis Gonzalez's soft blooper, normally an easy catch for Derek Jeter, a World Series-winning single over the shortstop's head.

Shockingly, Brenly sent Kim back out to the hill for the 10th inning. Clearly fatigued, Kim gave up an opposite-field fly ball to Derek Jeter that just barely cleared the right-field fence for a walk-off home run. With the Oct. 31 game having crept well past midnight, Jeter earned the nickname "Mr. November" from ecstatic Yankees fans.

135

Mays

GIANTS VS. INDIANS 1954 WORLD SERIES, GAME 1

AFTER A DOMINANT REGULAR SEASON IN WHICH THEY SNAPPED THE YANKS' streak of five pennants, the Cleveland Indians were expected to easily win the 1954 World Series. They already had 111 wins, an AL single-season record, and 14 more than their opponents, the New York Giants. But the first game was close. Tied, 2-2, in the eighth, the Indians led off with a walk and a single. With lefty slugger Vic Wertz due up, New York called on lefty reliever Don Liddle. Wertz clubbed the first pitch more than 450 feet to center — a definite homer in most parks. But the center-field fence at New York's Polo Grounds was 483 feet away.

Giants center fielder Willie Mays sprinted toward the wall, seeming to instinctively know where the ball would drop. He made the catch over his shoulder on the dead run. "I thought I had that one all the way," he said. Although the ball was likely deep enough for Larry Doby to tag and score from second, Mays quickly turned and threw, holding him at third and keeping the game tied. Liddle, who had thrown one pitch, was relieved by Marv Grissom. "Well, I got my man," Liddle cracked, walking off the field. The Giants won the game in 10 and went on to sweep the vaunted Indians.

Johnson
(right)

Griffey

PIRATES VS. SENATORS
1925 WORLD SERIES, GAME 7

ALTHOUGH A NASTY STORM WAS POURING RAIN
on Pittsburgh's Forbes Field, Commissioner Kenesaw Mountain
Landis demanded the Pirates and Senators play Game 7 of the
1925 World Series. The shoddy conditions resulted in what one
writer called "the wettest, weirdest, and wildest game that 50 years
of baseball has ever seen … "

With his fielders slipping and sliding on the field, Washington's
Walter Johnson gave up six runs to the Pirates, but he still led, 7-6,
in the eighth when Pittsburgh threatened. With bases loaded and
two outs, the Pirates' Kiki Cuyler flied to right; ruled a ground-rule
double, the hit gave Pittsburgh the runs that would win the Series.

REDS VS. RED SOX
1975 WORLD SERIES, GAME 7

THE MOMENTUM OF THE 1975 WORLD SERIES
swung toward Boston after Carlton Fisk's dramatic Game 6 homer,
and the Sox scored the first three runs of Game 7 the next day.
But they would be held there by Reds starter Don Gullett and
relievers Jack Billingham, Clay Carroll and Will McEnaney. A
sixth-inning homer from Tony Perez off a Bill Lee blooper pitch
cut the deficit to 3-2. The Reds tied it in the seventh and grabbed
the lead in the ninth when Boston reliever Jim Burton broke down.
After Ken Griffey and Pete Rose drew walks, Joe Morgan singled in
the winning run with two down. Quipped Lee: "After the game,
Gullett will go to the Hall of Fame, and I'll go to Eliot's Lounge."

WORLD SERIES

Spiezio

RALLY MONKEY

ANGELS VS. GIANTS 2002 WORLD SERIES, GAME 6

NEARLY HALF A CENTURY AFTER LEAVING Harlem for the West Coast, the San Francisco Giants were still without a world championship. They had come close in 1962, only to follow that with four decades of disappointment. In 2002 they roared back, surrounding the greatest hitter of the era, Barry Bonds, with a supporting cast of veterans that enabled the Giants to take a 3-games-to-2 lead over the Angels in the World Series. In Game 6, San Francisco held a 5-0 advantage in the seventh, but starter Russ Ortiz tired and was relieved by Felix Rodriguez, who immediately gave up a three-run homer to Anaheim's Scott Spiezio.

In the eighth, the Angels' Darin Erstad — hardly a power hitter — crushed a leadoff home run to cut the Giants' lead to 5-4. When the next two batters also reached base, San Francisco turned to Robb Nen for the save. But Troy Glaus hit one into the left-center-field gap over Bonds' head, scoring the tying and go-ahead runs. "I was just trying to have him hit the ball on the ground," the shell-shocked Nen said. Although Anaheim's rally fizzled out after Glaus' double, the one-run lead proved enough when closer Troy Percival retired the side in the ninth to force a Game 7.

"It was a great ballgame," Angels Manager Mike Scioscia said. "When you have two teams with a passion to strive for something, there are always special things that can happen." The Angels won the Series the next night, and Glaus was named World Series MVP.

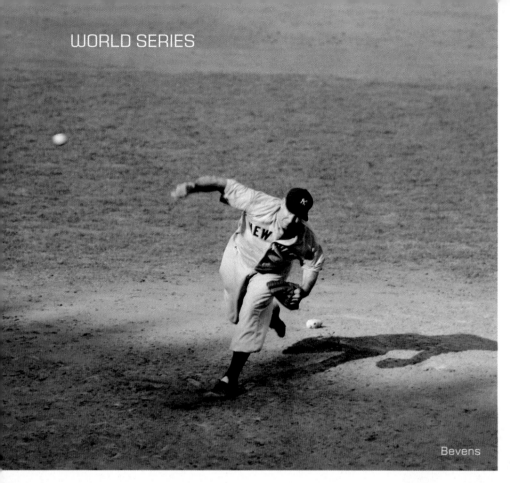

Bevens

DODGERS VS. YANKEES 1947 WORLD SERIES, GAME 4

ON OCT. 3, 1947, AN OBSCURE right-handed Yankee sought immortality by almost throwing a World Series no-hitter against the Brooklyn Dodgers. Floyd "Bill" Bevens, a 30-year-old with in-and-out control, led the Dodgers, 2-1, entering the bottom of the ninth in Game 4. Brooklyn put the winning run on base, and with two outs pinch-hitter Cookie Lavagetto hit to the opposite field. The drive flew over the glove of leaping right fielder Tommy Henrich, who allowed the game-winning run to score with the grand attempt. With one swing, Lavagetto had ended the no-no and won the game. After the Series ended, neither he nor Bevens would see the Majors again.

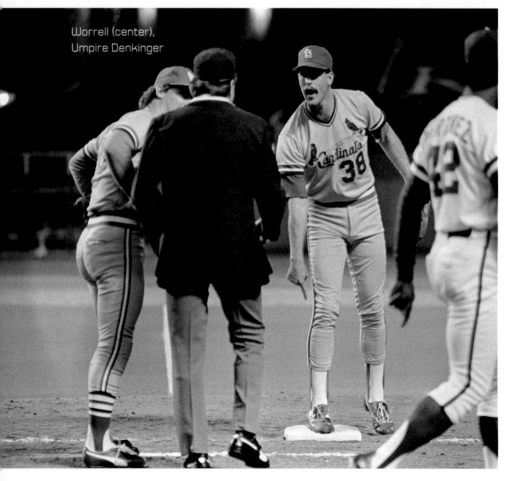

Worrell (center), Umpire Denkinger

ROYALS VS. CARDINALS 1985 WORLD SERIES, GAME 6

IN 1985, ST. LOUIS FIELDED ITS best team in decades — a slick-fielding, speedy club that overwhelmed opponents with stolen bases and turf-aided hits. As the Cards entered the ninth inning of Game 6, they were just three outs from a world championship. Leading off the inning, the Royals' Jorge Orta bounced a grounder to first. Jack Clark fielded the ball and tossed to rookie reliever Todd Worrell covering the bag. The throw beat Orta by half a step, but he was called safe by Umpire Don Denkinger. The Royals then mounted a rally, scoring twice to win the game. "The two best teams are in the World Series," Manager Whitey Herzog said. "They ought to have the best umpires in it, too. I think it's a disgrace." Kansas City trounced the Cards, 11-0, in Game 7, and the still-enraged Herzog was ejected to boot.

CARDINALS VS. TIGERS 1968 WORLD SERIES, GAME 1

LIKE WORLD RECORDS IN SWIMMING OR TRACK, the World Series single-game strikeout record seemed to be broken every few years. First was Deacon Phillippe with 10; then Bill Dinneen with 11; Ed Walsh, Bill Donovan and Walter Johnson with 12, Howard Ehmke with 13; Carl Erskine with 14; and Sandy Koufax with 15. But in '68 Bob Gibson not only enjoyed one of the most dominant seasons ever but also capped it off by setting a Fall Classic strikeout record that would finally stand the test of time.

Gibson mowed down 17 Tigers in Game 1, including sluggers Al Kaline and Norm Cash three times each, as the Cards beat Detroit, 4-0. Gibson eclipsed Koufax's record by whiffing the last three batters,

including Willie Horton, to end it. "He struck out quite a few with that … curveball," Tigers batting coach Wally Moses said. "Then he has that hard slider and the real good fastball. And control."

Gibson, for his part, was so intense that he claimed to have missed the congratulatory message on the scoreboard — not even realizing he had broken a record. "I just want outs, I just want to win the game," he said. "I wasn't aware of anything special." Said Tigers Manager Mayo Smith: "When a pitcher is like that, the hitters are just not going to get him. But we'll show up tomorrow. There'll be no forfeits in this Series." Although Gibson shattered his own 1964 record with 35 Ks in the Series, the Tigers would take the championship.

chapter 14
HEARTSTRINGS

Baseball is no stranger to moments of high drama, but sometimes the backstory is as important as the game itself. Whether it's Lou Gehrig's Yankee Stadium farewell or Roberto Clemente's 3,000th hit, the human side of the game tends to bring out emotion in everyone. Take the case of Bert Shepard. A Minor League pitcher in the early 1940s, Shepard, like so many of his peers, served in World War II. A fighter pilot, he was shot down over Germany and had his right leg amputated after the crash. But that didn't stop him from fulfilling his dream. Outfitted with an artificial limb, Shepard threw 5.1 innings of one-run ball in his Major League debut with the Senators.

JACKIE ROBINSON APRIL 15, 1947

ALMOST ALL ROOKIES GET NERVOUS ABOUT their Major League debuts, hoping not to embarrass themselves and wondering whether they'll prove they belong. But never was a first game as monumental or nerve-wracking as Jackie Robinson's first game for the Brooklyn Dodgers. When he took the field on April 15, 1947, trotting out to first base in the top of the first inning, he became the first African-American to play in the modern era of Major League Baseball. Robinson knew he would be watched closely not only by teammates and opponents, but by the press, by racists who opposed his playing and most importantly, by a nation of African-Americans ardently rooting for him. A crowd of 25,623 fans filtered into Ebbets Field that day, an estimated 14,000 of them were black. Robinson tried to take to heart the words of

Dodgers President Branch Rickey, who knew Jackie's talent would eventually shine through. "I want you to run wild, steal the pants off them, to be the most conspicuous player on the field," Rickey had told him.

Robinson faced the Braves' Johnny Sain in his first at-bat and grounded out to third. Despite going 0 for 3 in that game, he scored Brooklyn's winning run after bunting and running down the baseline so furiously that a rushed infielder threw the ball away. Jackie struggled throughout April, but by May he had become one of the best and most respected players in the National League. He would go on to be named Rookie of the Year at the end of the season. Even his most ardent opponent, segregationist and Phillies Manager Ben Chapman, was forced to admit that Robinson "is a Major Leaguer in every respect."

CAL RIPKEN JR.
SEPTEMBER 6, 1995

AS SOON AS THE 1995 SCHEDULE was released, fans circled Sept. 6 on their calendars — the date Cal Ripken would likely break Lou Gehrig's seemingly untouchable record by playing in his 2,131st consecutive game. Although Ripken never had a nickname like "The Iron Horse," his streak was undeniably more impressive than Gehrig's. Ripken played the demanding position of shortstop, and unlike Gehrig, he appeared in virtually every minute of every game, shattering the Major League record for consecutive innings played. Ripken did not extend his streak on a technicality either, as an injured Gehrig once did in 1934. (Gehrig batted in the first inning of a game and was then taken out, never seeing the field.)

That night, against the Angels at Camden Yards, Ripken rose to the occasion by hitting a homer in the fourth inning. A half inning later the game became official, and Ripken's record was in the books. Cal was feted by dignitaries, including President Bill Clinton, as a "2131" banner was unfurled on the face of the B & O Warehouse in right field. The fans rewarded their hero with a 22-minute standing ovation. Ripken embarked on an emotional victory lap, jogging around the edges of the field, slapping hands with fans in the front rows. "Cal was trying to let it die a little bit," teammate Bobby Bonilla told the *Baltimore Sun*. "That's how Cal is. He wasn't going to do anything to add to it. [But] they wanted more of Cal. Everybody was so caught up in the whole thing."

Greenberg

HANK GREENBERG &
JACKIE ROBINSON
MAY 15, 1947

ALTHOUGH JACKIE ROBINSON ENDURED MUCH bigotry in 1947, he wasn't the first. "There was nobody in the history of the game who took more abuse than [Hank] Greenberg, unless it was Jackie Robinson," Greenberg's teammate Birdie Tebbetts said. During the World Series of 1935, Greenberg, one of baseball's first Jewish stars, was heckled so badly that three Cubs, including Manager Charlie Grimm, were ejected. In '47, the only season the two players shared the field, Greenberg became one of Jackie's biggest supporters. "Stick in there," Greenberg told him the first time they met. "You're doing fine. Keep your chin up." Robinson greatly admired Greenberg, and never forgot the encouragement. "Class tells," Robinson said. "It sticks out all over Mr. Greenberg."

145

MIKE PIAZZA   SEPTEMBER 21, 2001

THE TERRORIST ATTACKS OF SEPT. 11 SHOOK THE nation to its core. As America's pastime took a week's hiatus to allow the country to mourn and recover, the New York Mets had a closer view of the devastation than most. Shea Stadium's parking lot became a temporary NYPD command center, and the ballpark was used as a site to store food and clothing that was collected for relief efforts. Although the Mets had been on the road when the tragedy occurred, they got a view of the horrific scene when their team bus crossed the George Washington Bridge while heading back into New York on Sept. 12. "We've all come to realize we're now living in a different world," said team President David Howard.

Many Mets used the week off to help the relief efforts at Shea, while others visited injured survivors at local hospitals. Mike Piazza, for one, looked forward to resuming play, because it would give him

something to keep his mind off the tragedy. "You have to get back to some sort of routine in order to be productive and keep your mind from succumbing to depression," Piazza said. "You cannot fall into that trap." On Sept. 21, the Mets hosted the rival Braves in Shea's first post-9/11 game, and the Mets showed their support for city workers by wearing NYPD and FDNY caps as part of their uniform.

The environment at Shea was part wake and part revival, as bagpipes played "Amazing Grace" before the game. The ceremony gave way to rousing exhortations of "U.S.A.!" and a seventh-inning stretch rendition of "New York, New York" by Liza Minnelli. Atlanta looked as if it had victory in hand, but in the eighth inning Piazza delivered a small measure of happiness to New Yorkers by hitting a dramatic two-run homer for a come-from-behind victory for the Mets.

TED WILLIAMS SEPTEMBER 28, 1960

ON SEPT. 28, 1960, A PALTRY CROWD OF 10,454 ENTERED Fenway Park to see off another disappointing Red Sox season. More importantly, though, they were there to salute Ted Williams one last time. The greatest player in franchise history, Williams was retiring with 520 homers and 1,838 RBI. The love-hate relationship Williams had long endured with Boston fans was forgotten as they cheered wildly every time he came to bat. In the bottom of the eighth, Williams dug into the Fenway batter's box for the final time, and crushed a pitch 420 feet over the center-field wall.

Appropriately, for a game played in America's literary capital, Williams' triumphant farewell was treated like the last-whispered words of a dying king. Most famously, John Updike used the home run as a stepping-off point for an essay about The Kid's career and its importance to New England. "The ball seemed less an object in flight than the tip of a towering, motionless construct, like the Eiffel Tower or the Tappan Zee Bridge," Updike wrote. "He ran as he always ran out home runs — hurriedly, unsmiling, head down, as if our praise were a storm of rain to get out of." The game was delayed for several minutes as Red Sox Nation chanted Williams' name and exhorted him to take a curtain call. But Teddy Ballgame, perhaps mindful of past slights by the fans, refused to come out of the dugout. As Updike wrote, "Gods do not answer letters."

Murcer (second
from right)

BOBBY MURCER AUGUST 6, 1979

AS TURMOIL ENGULFED THE YANKEES IN THE LATE 1970s, it was no-nonsense team captain Thurman Munson who kept things sane. A seven-time All-Star, three-time Gold Glove winner and 1976 AL MVP, Munson ignored the animosities among Reggie Jackson, Billy Martin and others, and concentrated on playing instead. "He was not one to sit back and hotdog," said Rev. J. Robert Coleman, Munson's pastor. "You knew where you stood with Thurman Munson."

The catcher was learning to fly so he could visit his family in Canton, Ohio, on off days. While practicing takeoffs and landings at the Canton airport on Aug. 2, 1979, Munson crashed his twin-engine plane and died. After attending Munson's funeral in Ohio on Aug. 6, the Yankees flew back to New York for a night game against Baltimore. Although nobody wanted to play, they took the field anyway. "If he was sitting here and I said I couldn't play, he'd say, 'You're crazy,'" Bobby Murcer said. So the Yankees played. "The first time I got out to the mound and looked around," said that night's pitcher, Ron Guidry, "there was something missing." Guidry fell behind, 4-0, but in the seventh inning Murcer smacked a three-run homer to make it 4-3. Murcer came up again in the ninth, and with runners on second and third he knocked a walk-off single for a 5-4 Yankees victory. Munson would have loved it.

chapter 15

WHAT A GAME!

Whether they were in the ballpark or saw it on television, every single baseball fan has experienced one of those games. You know — one when the stars align to produce a contest that transcends baseball. Like a captivating novel, each page contains a moment of beauty or a shocking surprise. Such games amaze even those playing in them. During Game 6 of the 1975 World Series — the epic ended by Carlton Fisk — Pete Rose came to bat in the 10th inning, turned to Fisk and said, "I don't know about you, but this is the greatest game I ever played in."

PAWTUCKET RED SOX VS. ROCHESTER RED WINGS
APRIL 18, 1981

WHEN THE ROCHESTER RED WINGS AND the Pawtucket Red Sox took the field on Saturday night, April 18, 1981, they hoped for a quick game. It was bitterly cold at Pawtucket's McCoy Stadium, and the players were anxious to get home and rest for their day game on Easter Sunday. "I'll never forget how cold it was, and how hard the wind was blowing," PawSox second baseman Marty Barrett told *The Washington Post.* "We all wanted the night to go real fast." Instead, they got the longest game in professional baseball history — a game so long that Rochester's Cal Ripken Jr., who went 2 for 13, joked, "a lot of us had a bad week that day." It was a game so long that Pawtucket third baseman Wade Boggs was 22 years old when it began and 23 when it ended.

The Red Wings led, 1-0, heading into the bottom of the ninth but the PawSox evened it up to send the game into extra frames. Eleven scoreless innings followed, despite a near walk-off home run by Pawtucket's Sam Bowen that was blown back onto the field at the last

second by a gust of wind. In the 21st, Rochester finally scored the go-ahead run, only for Pawtucket to tie it up on a Boggs double. "By around [midnight or 1 a.m.], it seemed like a lot of us got our second wind," Barrett said. "But then all of a sudden, you hit a wall. By 4, we were almost delirious." Finally at 4:07 a.m., the league president, who was reached at home, suspended the game in the 32nd inning. "It's the only time I ever remember our postgame meal being breakfast," Ripken said.

The game resumed on June 23 before a sellout crowd and a national media throng, and took just 18 minutes to end. "Bases loaded, nobody out, and Wade Boggs on deck," said Dave Koza, who got the winning hit for Pawtucket. "There was no pressure on me." Koza's single to left ended the game after 33 innings, 219 at-bats and 882 pitches. Steve Grilli, Rochester's losing pitcher, had been with another organization when the game began. "What it took them eight-and-a-half hours to accomplish," he said, "I undid in about two minutes."

PROVIDENCE GRAYS VS. DETROIT WOLVERINES
AUGUST 17, 1882

IN 1882, THE GAME OF BASEBALL first started to look like the game we know today, at least from a sartorial perspective. It was the first season that National League teams sported specific uniform colors. Wearing light blue and gold, respectively, the Providence Grays and the Detroit Wolverines staged what one reporter called "the best contested game of base ball on record." It was a game in which the batting hero was a future Hall of Fame pitcher and the pitching hero was a future Hall of Fame batter.

On Aug. 17, at the Messer Street Grounds in Providence, Grays pitcher John Ward (who would later be converted into a star shortstop) matched zeroes for 17 innings with Detroit ace Stump Wiedman, who had recorded a league-best 1.80 ERA the previous season. Ward finally was rescued by Charles "Old Hoss" Radbourn, the Providence Grays' other pitcher, who played the outfield on his off days despite a horrid .235 career batting average. "Amid tremendous excitement Radbourne [sic] drove the ball over the fence for four bases in the 18th inning and won the longest game on record in the league," one observer noted. Although his remarkable 201 strikeouts would lead the major leagues that season, it was Radbourn's first career homer. Over the course of the century many games have lasted longer, but nobody ever has surpassed Ward's 18-inning, complete-game shutout.

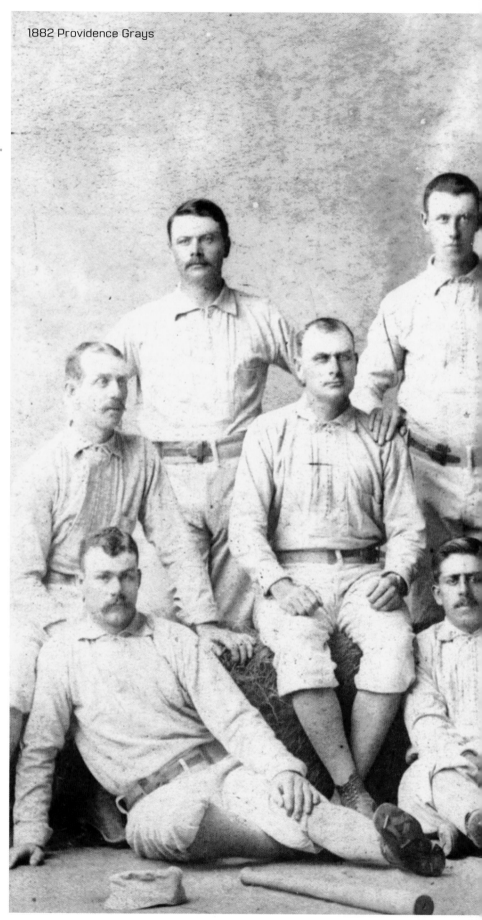

1882 Providence Grays

Munro

HOUSTON ASTROS JUNE 11, 2003

MAKING HIS FIRST START IN YANKEE STADIUM ON June 11, 2003, Roy Oswalt cruised through the first frame. But in the second, he aggravated a nagging groin injury, and had to leave the game after just 24 pitches. Oswalt hoped his bullpen would pick him up — and, boy, did it ever. Although his replacement, Peter Munro, struggled with his control, he safely navigated through 2.2 innings without allowing a hit. In

the fifth, soft-tossing right-hander Kirk Saarloos took over for Munro, tacking on another 1.1 hitless innings. Saarloos then gave the ball to rookie flamethrower Brad Lidge, who tossed two perfect innings of his own.

Despite holding a 6-0 lead, Astros skipper Jimy Williams managed the game like a nail-biter, opting to send set-up man Octavio Dotel out for the eighth and closer Billy Wagner for the

JOE DiMAGGIO JULY 17, 1941

INDIANS THIRD BASEMAN KEN KELTNER HAD A borderline Hall of Fame career, making seven All-Star teams and receiving MVP votes in five seasons, but he's remembered today for one thing: halting Joe DiMaggio's 56-game hitting streak at Cleveland Municipal Stadium on July 17, 1941.

In DiMaggio's first at-bat against lefty Al Smith, he grounded down the third-base line. Ordinarily, it would have been a double, but Keltner, playing deep, was able to snag it and throw DiMaggio out from the lip of the outfield grass. Next time up, Smith walked DiMaggio. In his third try, Joltin' Joe crushed another hard grounder down the line, but again Keltner was positioned masterfully. DiMaggio got one final chance in the eighth, with the bases loaded and Jim Bagby Jr. on the mound. He hit a grounder to short that looked as if it might bounce into the outfield, but shortstop Lou Boudreau reacted quickly, turning a double play. A rally in the ninth might have given DiMaggio another chance, but it never materialized. The streak was dead at 56. "I can't say that I'm glad it's over," DiMaggio admitted. "Now that the streak is over, I just want to get out there and keep helping to win ball games."

ninth. Dotel tied a record by striking out four in his inning, with the second batter of the frame, Alfonso Soriano, reaching on a wild pitch. When Wagner, who needed just 14 pitches to shut the door on the Yankees in the ninth, pumped his fist in joy, teammate Jeff Kent hadn't even realized there was a no-hitter in progress. Nevertheless, the six Astros hurlers made history; no team had ever pitched a no-hitter using more than four pitchers.

BIBLIOGRAPHY

BOOKS and JOURNALS:

Cramer, Richard Ben. *Joe DiMaggio: The Hero's Life*. New York: Simon & Schuster, 2000.

Creamer, Robert W. *Babe: The Legend Comes to Life*. New York: Simon & Schuster, 1974.

Enders, Eric. *The Fall Classic: The Definitive History of the World Series*. New York: Sterling, 2007.

Greenberg, Hank, with Ira Berkow. *Hank Greenberg: The Story of My Life*. New York: Crown, 1989.

Halberstam, David. *Summer of '49*. New York: William Morrow, 1991.

Holway, John. *The Complete Book of Baseball's Negro Leagues*. Fern Park, FL: Hastings House, 2001.

Jones, David, editor. *Deadball Stars of the American League*. Dulles, VA: Potomac, 2006.

Kashatus, William C. *Mike Schmidt: Philadelphia's Hall of Fame Third Baseman*. Jefferson, NC: McFarland & Co., 1999.

Kelley, Brent P. *I Will Never Forget: Interviews With 39 Former Negro League Players*. Jefferson, NC: McFarland & Co., 2003.

Liebman, Glenn. *Grand Slams!: The Ultimate Collection of Baseball's Best Quips, Quotes, and Cutting Remarks*. New York: McGraw-Hill, 2001.

Montville, Leigh. *Ted Williams: The Biography of an American Hero*. New York: Broadway, 2005.

Peary, Danny. *We Played the Game*. New York: Hyperion, 1994.

Ribowsky, Mark. *Don't Look Back: Satchel Paige in the Shadows of Baseball*. Cambridge, MA: Da Capo, 2000.

Ritter, Lawrence. *The Glory of Their Times*. New York: William Morrow, 1984.

Sahlins, Marshall David. *Apologies to Thucydides: Understanding History as Culture and Vice Versa*. Chicago: University of Chicago Press, 1994.

Simon, Tom, editor. *Deadball Stars of the National League*. Dulles, VA: Brassey's, 2006.

Snyder, Brad. *Beyond the Shadow of the Senators: The Untold Story of the Homestead Grays and the Integration of Baseball*. New York: McGraw-Hill, 2003.

Thomas, Henry. *Walter Johnson: Baseball's Big Train*. Arlington, VA: Phenom Press, 2005.

Veeck, Bill, with Ed Linn. *Veeck: As In Wreck*. Chicago: University of Chicago Press, 2001.

Witt, Jessica K., and Dennis R. Proffitt. "*See the Ball, Hit the Ball: Apparent Ball Size is Correlated with Batting Average*." Psychological Science, Volume 16, Issue 12, December 2005.

MAGAZINES and NEWSPAPERS:

Countless issues of the following magazines and newspapers were used as reference material in researching *Baseball's Greatest Games*.

At the Yard

Baltimore Sun

Baseball Digest

Boston Globe

Chicago Tribune

Dallas Morning News

Detroit News

Los Angeles Times

Nevada Appeal

New York Times

Oakland Tribune

Oxnard Press-Courier

Rocky Mountain News

Sports Illustrated

Syracuse Post-Standard

Wall Street Journal

Washington Post

Wausheka Daily Freeman

WEBSITES:

www.baseball-reference.com

www.baseballguru.com

www.baseballhalloffame.org

www.baseballlibrary.com

www.cbc.ca

www.latimes.com

www.minorleaguebaseball.com

www.mlb.com

www.newspaperarchive.com

www.retrosheet.org

www.sabr.org

PHOTO CREDITS:

TOM DIPACE/MLB PHOTOS: 8-9 (Jones)

BASEBALL HALL OF FAME: 11 (Dillon); 14 (Duggleby); 19 (Cross); 31 (Ruth); 40 (Richmond); 48 (Paige); 52 (Foster); 56 (Oeschger); 57 (Toney); 61 (Joss); 62-63 (Wood); 67 (Merkle);

150-151 (Rochester vs. Pawtucket); 127 (Athletics vs. Giants); 127 (Red Sox vs. Giants); 152-153 (Providence)

AP: 10: (Holloman); 30 (Baines); 35 (Stennett); 39 (Larsen); 59 (Haddix); 68-69 (Gaedel); 90 (Clarke); 91 (Ring); 92 (Williams); 93 (Jackson); 94 (Callison); 110-111 (Smith); 114 (Chambliss); 122 (Browns vs. White Stockings); 122 (Cardinals vs. Yankees); 124 (Athletics vs. Cubs); 149 (Yankees)

DENNIS DESPROIS: 12-13 (Clark); 136 (Giants vs. Indians)

BETTMANN/CORBIS: 15 (Gray); 16-17 (Feller); 22-23 (Mays); 25 (Schmidt); 58 (Marichal); 64-65 (Brett); 66 (Hartnett); 80-81 (Dent); 86 (Chicago Colts); 100-101 (Boston Red Sox); 126 (Cardinals vs. Red Sox); 133 (Braves vs. Yankees); 140 (Dodgers vs. Yankees); 140 (Royals vs. Cardinals); 141 (Cardinals vs. Tigers); 142-143 (Robinson); 148 (Williams); 155 (DiMaggio)

BILL LIVINGSTON/MLB PHOTOS: 18 (Valenzuela)

LOUIS REQUENA/MLB PHOTOS: 21 (Jackson); 41 (Hunter)

WIDE WORLD PHOTOS/ASSOCIATED PRESS: 24 (Lowe)

SKEOCH/ MLB PHOTOS: 26-27 (Delgado)

MIRALLE /ALLSPORT/GETTY IMAGES: 28-29 (Tatis)

AP PHOTO/TED SANDE: 32 (Williams)

RON VESELY/MLB PHOTOS: 34 (Whiten)

ROBERT BECK/MLB PHOTOS: 35 (Green)

FSU SPORTS INFORMATION: 35 (McDougall)

AP PHOTO/JOHN BAZEMORE: 42-43 (Johnson)

CRANDALL ASSOCIATES/MLB PHOTOS: 44 (Cone)

CORBIS: 45 (Shore)

AP PHOTO/LENNY IGNELZI: 47 (Hershiser)

DANIEL LIPPITT/AFP/GETTY IMAGES: 49 (Wood)

AP PHOTO/ANTHONY CAMERANO: 50-51 (Vander Meer)

AP PHOTO/DAVID ZALUBOWSKI: 53 (Nomo)

MLB PHOTOS: 54 (Morris); 130-131 (Pirates vs. Yankees)

AP PHOTO/NATIONAL BASEBALL HALL OF FAME LIBRARY: 60 (Williams)

AP PHOTO/MARK LENNIHAN: 70 (Orioles vs. Yankees)

ELSA/GETTY IMAGES: 71 (Marlins vs. Cubs)

SHAW/GETTY IMAGES: 72-73 (Ortiz)

PHOTO FILE/GETTY IMAGES: 74 (Thomson)

MYER OSTROFF/CORBIS: 76 (DiMaggio)

DAVID BERGMAN/CORBIS: 77 (Boone)

RONALD C. MODRA/SPORTS IMAGERY/GETTY IMAGES: 78-79 (Sandberg)

ROBERT RIGER/GETTY IMAGES: 82-83 (Mays)

AP PHOTO/NICK WASS: 84-85 (Texas Rangers)

RICK STEWART/GETTY IMAGES: 87 (Toronto Blue Jays)

JEFF GROSS/GETTY IMAGES: 88-89 (Los Angeles Dodgers)

ALLEN KEE/MLB PHOTOS: 95-96 (Blalock)

DOUG PENSINGER/GETTY IMAGES: 98 (Colorado Rockies); 144-145 (Ripken Jr.)

ACME/CORBIS: 100 (Detroit Tigers)

NBLA/MLB PHOTOS: 102-103 (Detroit Tigers)

AP PHOTO/ERIC GAY: 104-105 (Astros vs. Braves)

JOHN G. MABANGLO/AFP/GETTY IMAGES: 106-107 (Yankees vs. Athletics)

BEN VAN HOUTEN: 108-109 (Griffey Jr.)

RONALD C. MODRA/SPORTS IMAGERY/ GETTY IMAGES: 112-113 (Bream)

JEFF HAYNES/AFP/GETTY IMAGES: 115 (Fernandez); 138 (Angels vs. Giants)

AP PHOTO/RAY STUBBLEBINE: 117 (Orosco)

AP PHOTO/RUSTY KENNEDY: 118 (Monday)

FOCUS ON SPORT/GETTY IMAGES: 119 (Bench); 128 (Mets vs. Red Sox); 137 (Reds vs. Red Sox)

RICH PILLING/MLB PHOTOS: 119 (Maddox)

WILL HART/GETTY IMAGES: 120-121 (Dodgers vs. Athletics)

MIKE BLAKE/REUTER/CORBIS: 123 (Blue Jays vs. Phillies)

GARY HERSHORN/REUTERS/CORBIS: 125 (Marlins vs. Indians)

AP PHOTO/HARRY CABLUCK: 129 (Red Sox vs. Reds)

HENRY GROSKINSKY/TIME LIFE PICTURES/GETTY IMAGES: 132 (Senators vs. Giants)

UPI/CORBIS: 133 (Yankees vs. Giants)

MANGIN/MLB PHOTOS: 134-135 (Yankees vs. Diamondbacks); 135 (Diamondbacks vs. Yankees)

MARK RUCKER/TRANSCENDENTAL GRAPHICS, GETTY IMAGES: 137 (Pirates vs. Senators)

KIDWILER COLLECTION/DIAMOND IMAGES/GETTY IMAGES: 145 (Greenberg)

REUTERS/CORBIS: 146-147 (Mets)

AP PHOTO/OSAMU HONDA: 154-155 (Astros)

ARTIFACT CREDITS:

ALL ARTIFACTS COURTESY OF MILO STEWART/ NATIONAL BASEBALL HALL OF FAME AND MUSEUM

INDEX